Guerrilla Music Marketing Handbook

201 Self-Promotion Ideas for Songwriters, Musicians and Bands on a Budget

Bob Baker

Spotlight Publications

www.TheBuzzFactor.com

St. Louis, MO

To Jay Conrad Levinson, the godfather of Guerrilla Marketing.

Thanks for shining the light, blazing a new trail, and inspiring millions (including me) to take the guerrilla path less traveled!

Published by Spotlight Publications and TheBuzzFactor.com

PO Box 28441, St. Louis, MO 63146 USA

© 2013 by Bob Baker

ISBN-10: 0-9714838-9-2

ISBN-13: 978-0-9714838-9-7

Disclaimer

About the author

Bob Baker is the author of the highly acclaimed *Guerrilla Music Marketing* series of books and several other titles, including *Branding Yourself Online* and *Unleash the Artist Within*. He also developed the "Music Marketing 101" course at Berkleemusic, the online continuing education division of Berklee College of Music.

Bob is a musician, visual artist, actor, and former music magazine editor who is dedicated to showing musicians of all kinds how to get exposure, connect with fans, sell more music, and increase their incomes through their artistic passions.

Since 1995 Bob has published "The Buzz Factor" ezine, one of the first music tips email newsletters in existence. He was one of the early proponents of musicians taking their careers into their own hands and not relying on major record labels or industry gatekeepers to save them. Bob is on a mission to empower artists using his articles, ezine, blog, podcast, and video clips.

Visit www.TheBuzzFactor.com for more details.

Other books and resources by Bob Baker:

Guerrilla Music Marketing Online: 129 Free and Low-Cost Strategies to Promote & Sell Your Music on the Internet

Guerrilla Music Marketing, Encore Edition: 201 MORE Self-Promotion Ideas, Tips & Tactics for Do-It-Yourself Artists

Killer Music Press Kits: The 29 Most Important Elements in Creating Sizzling Music Publicity Materials

The Music Publicity Insider's Guide: How to Use News Hooks & Story Ideas to Get Media Exposure

Contents

Section 4: Guerrilla Music Money & Sales

Section 5: Guerrilla Music Promotion Tactics

Introduction

I have no way of knowing why you picked up this book or how you found it, but I do know one thing with total certainty: This is the best time in human history to be a musician!

You live in an amazing era. Artists of all stripes the world over are taking their talents and empowering themselves to build their own fan bases, book their own gigs, sell their own music and merchandise, and create business models that work for them.

It's an exciting time to be an independent (also known as "indie") musician and not have to rely on A&R big shots, record labels, or "the industry" to rescue you from obscurity. Today, you can rescue yourself and build your own music career – and you can do it on your own terms!

Old habits are hard to shake

For decades, aspiring musicians thought the only legitimate route to success was landing a recording contract with a major label. It was also assumed that a new band needed to be on commercial radio and in major retail outlets to have a fighting chance to survive.

The times have definitely changed. The Internet and low-cost recording technologies have created a thriving do-it-yourself music movement with unlimited options to get exposure and reach fans. Unfortunately, thousands of songwriters and artists still believe the road to widespread recognition can only be traveled through a record deal.

My advice: *Wake up and smell the gigabytes!*

I believe the best way to approach a career as a musician (especially one who writes and performs original music) is to take control, get your hands dirty, and market your music yourself. No one will ever feel as strongly about your craft as you do. Which means you're the best person in the world to spread the news.

Sure, promoting your own music takes a lot of effort. No doubt. But it's well worth it. And despite what you may have heard to the contrary, it can be profitable.

Artists who have succeeded on their own terms

Here are several inspiring examples of self-empowered musicians:

- **Loreena McKennitt** has sold more than 14 million of her "eclectic Celtic" albums worldwide. Her independent music career spans eight studio recordings and one double-live album. She is completely self-managed, self-produced, and the head of her own internationally successful record label, Quinlan Road (www.quinlanroad.com).

McKennitt's music has won critical acclaim and gold, platinum and multi-platinum sales awards in 15 countries across four continents. She continues to manage her own career to this day.

- In 1988, **Lorie Line** (www.lorieline.com) got a job playing piano for customers at a Dayton's department store in Minneapolis. Little did she know it would lead to Lorie Line Music, Inc., a family-run business that has released 36 albums, with sales exceeding 6 million copies. She has also published 28 complete books of piano music.

Line attributes her success to the basics – hard work, talent, perseverance, and gut instincts. She is involved with every aspect of her company: management, sales, direct mail, public relations, marketing, tour scheduling, website management, and music creation.

"It's hard to believe that the company I started in my basement is now the second largest artist-owned record label in North America," she says. "People always ask me how we do it all by ourselves. It is overwhelming if you think about it too much. But, because I do something that I absolutely love, my job is rewarding and continually fun."

- Does the name **Mark Maxwell** (www.romanticsaxmusic.com) ring a bell? Perhaps not. But he's one of the best-selling saxophonists in the world. And although his name is not a household word, his 18 self-promoted solo releases have sold more than 500,000 copies (yes, half a million) without the support of a record label or significant radio airplay.

- **David Nevue** (www.davidnevue.com) quit a good-paying tech job in 2001 to become a full-time musician and author. The move wasn't exactly a risky one. Over the previous six years he had spent much of his spare time building awareness for his solo piano music on the Internet. Through hard work and persistence, he went from obscurity to being one of the most widely played independent New Age artists. He now has thousands of fans and supports his family from his various independent music activities. Nevue shares his secrets in a book called *How to Promote Your Music Successfully on the Internet*.

- The indie band **Clap Your Hands Say Yeah** used online buzz and word of mouth to sell 270,000 copies of its debut album. Guitarist Robbie Guertin told *Spin* magazine, "What can [a record label] do for us that we can't do ourselves? Maybe if someone came up with a good answer, we'd sign. But no one has yet."

- **John Taglieri** (www.johntaglieri.com) is a full-time singer/songwriter who had an entire chapter devoted to him in previous editions of this book. He is an independent music dynamo who completely embodies the principles of guerrilla music marketing. Over a 12-year period he sold 20,000 copies of his first 10 albums, played more than 3,000 live shows, and earned several Top 10 singles on Amazon.com. He spends half the year in Key West, FL, where he performs for huge crowds, and the other half touring the East Coast of the U.S. He runs his own recording studio and record label and is sponsored by Curt Mangan Strings, Ovation Guitars, and more.

- **Jack Conte** and **Nataly Dawn** (known as **Pomplamoose**) used quirky versions of popular cover songs to build a large fan base on YouTube. That attracted the attention of car companies that used their music in national TV commercials. The duo has turned down many record label offers and chooses to stay independent. Read more about their story in Chapter 8.

- **Amy Heidemann** and **Nick Noonan** of the duo **Karmin** also leveraged the popularity of YouTube cover song videos into a music career. Only they decided to go the major label route and have benefited from national TV exposure and Billboard pop chart success. But they earned their place in the music industry by embracing guerrilla music marketing tactics and an indie work ethic. See Chapter 8 for more on Karmin and their rise to fame.

- **Mark Mohr** is another name you have probably never heard of. Yet he makes a great living serving a musical genre called "gospel reggae," which he helped create more than 20 years ago. He tours the world profitably with a 10-piece band.

Make no mistake: It is possible to make your mark, make a difference, and even make a living creating and sharing your music. These artists have done it. And by honing your craft, focusing on fans, and putting smart marketing practices into action, you can do it too!

Doing it yourself

You've most likely heard of singer/songwriter Ani DiFranco. At age 20, she started her own label, Righteous Babe Records (www.righteousbabe.com), and began performing a growing number of solo acoustic shows. Coffeehouse gigs led to colleges, then larger theaters and major folk festivals.

DiFranco was one of the early indie music pioneers who, in the 1990s, accomplished all of her success without a major record label, commercial radio airplay, MTV exposure, or advertising. Over a two-decade period she has successfully released 20 albums, toured extensively, and made CMJ's list of the 25 most influential artists of the last 25 years. Along the way, she has inspired countless musicians to rewrite the rules of the recording industry and strive for self-sufficiency.

According to her bio, "Early in her career, Ani made a choice that is now so obvious to so many people that it's hard to remember it was once considered brazen: to say no to every record label deal that came her way, and yes to being her own boss."

So the next time you get down in the dumps because that major label recording contract hasn't come your way yet, pause and realize that – like DiFranco and other self-supporting musicians – you are better off as an independent artist.

Putting your music career in focus

This manual was written to help you get a grip on the confusing topics of music marketing, promotion and sales. The concepts, ideas and suggestions in these pages are simple. That's not to say they're always easy. There's work to be done here, but it's the kind of activity that's well within your ability to pull off.

The problem with most independent music people, even the ones who take lots of action, is that their efforts are unfocused and wasted on the wrong activities. By the time you finish reading and working with this book, you'll have a much clearer idea of how to direct your energies.

Here are five essential principles that run throughout these pages. If you understand them now you'll get a lot more out of this book:

1) **Question everything you've ever been told about the music business.** If you get involved in the music biz for long, you'll encounter plenty of people – some with impressive résumés – who will offer you their best music business advice. That's fine. The more information you take in, the better educated you'll be. But remain flexible and open-minded. The rules are changing quickly, so beware of anyone with an outdated, black-and-white view of the music world. These days, *you* get to pick and choose which existing "rules" truly apply to you – and you can create more empowering rules that suit you along the way.

2) **Give yourself permission to succeed.** The biggest mistake you can make is waiting for someone or something else to deem you worthy of pursuing a music career. You don't need an official sanction or a green light from anyone other than yourself (and the segment of the fan population you serve). So go ahead and give yourself approval right now!

3) **Whenever you take action to promote your music, you must know exactly why you're taking the action to begin with.** Action by itself is not enough. You must know the purpose behind your actions. What is the real outcome you desire? The best way to make sure you're going about things effectively is to come up with a plan that makes sense, have very focused goals, and realize that you need to provide a benefit (or solution) to everyone you connect with in the music business.

4) **Think outside of your mental box.** Human beings are creatures of habit. We become victims of our own routines. Therefore, it's no surprise that we slip into a narrow way of doing things. Habits are quite useful when they involve brushing your teeth, getting dressed, and driving a car.

   But when it comes to promoting your music, this routine way of thinking – and acting – is stunting your progress. When you market yourself the same way you've always done it, or the same way a thousand other artists have done it, you become part of the great music swamp in which everyone looks and sounds the same. Don't get lulled into monotony. Break those patterns!

5) **Have fun – marketing shouldn't be so damn serious!** There's a misguided belief that defeats most musicians before they even start promoting themselves. It's the notion that to market yourself effectively you have to shift into serious "business mode." That you have to be an expert in all facets of marketing strategy and not make any mistakes. No wonder so many artists are repulsed by marketing. I'm getting a headache just thinking about it now in those terms.

   To my way of thinking, marketing is simply a natural extension of the creative process. It's something you play with and experiment with to find the right combinations that work – similar to how you create music. Promotion should not be a burden. It should be energizing and enjoyable. You should bring a sense of playfulness and creativity to your marketing. Yes, when done right, you can actually have fun with it!

Your music marketing challenge

In this manual, I'll poke and prod you to be different, to expand your thinking, to focus your goals and actions – in essence, to become a true Guerrilla Music Marketer. We won't be talking about national advertising campaigns, arena tours, or worldwide retail distribution. Instead, the following pages will show you how to:

- Work from the trenches, with little or no money

- Use often-overlooked techniques to give your music wider exposure

- Build a following one fan at a time

- Use each small success as a stepping stone to a bigger and more significant accomplishment

I'm also going to ask you to think about these guerrilla marketing tactics and success stories and then capture the best ideas in a tangible form. For your convenience, I have created free downloadable worksheets you can use for this purpose. Just go to **worksheets.thebuzzfactor.com** to grab them now.

I implore you to use these worksheets! For it is here where my assorted suggestions come to life and become your own. By writing on these worksheets, you'll get a clearer idea of where you are and in what direction you need to be heading.

Guerrilla techniques in action

It was using these same guerrilla tactics – while capturing my thoughts and goals on paper – that led me to start playing guitar when I was 15. (The year was 1975, in case you're keeping score.) Over the decades since I have played thousands of gigs in venues big and small. I've done everything from playing in alternative rock and Top 40 bands to doing a lot of solo and duo work. I'm also a singer-songwriter who over the years has released several albums of original material.

In recent years most of my musical activities have been with my "very significant other," Pooki. She and I lead a rock and soul choir in St. Louis called Gateway to Agape. We also have a side music project called Soul Massage and play a few times a month at churches, small venues, and private parties.

Back in 1987 I launched my own local music magazine. I didn't have much money to work with and had no connections or experience with publishing. What I did have was a good concept and a knack for writing. I didn't let a lack of experience or credentials stop me. That newspaper, called *Spotlight*, grew and flourished for 10 years.

In 1993 a small publishing company put out my first book, *101 Ways to Make Money in the Music Business* (now out of print). Later that year I founded the St. Louis Regional Music Showcase, an annual music conference that ran for five years in the Midwest. In 1995 I self-published the first version of this very book you are reading now. I put the *Spotlight* newspaper to rest in 1997 so I could concentrate on becoming a full-time author, teacher and speaker.

Evolving over the years

In the mid 1990s I signed up for an AOL account (if you're old enough, you may remember when those free AOL floppy disks were everywhere). I had an email account for the first time and in 1995 started distributing my music marketing tips digitally. In those days I called it the "Musical Success Resource Guide." A few years later it evolved into *The Buzz Factor*, which I'm pretty sure is the longest-running music marketing tips email newsletter on the planet. I still send it out every month. You can subscribe for free at www.TheBuzzFactor.com.

As the Internet evolved, so did my methods of spreading the message. I have relentlessly shared my music advice through any channel that made sense. That's why you'll find many hundreds of posts on my blog (www.MusicPromotionBlog.com), Artist Empowerment Radio podcast (www.Bob-Baker.com/podcast) and YouTube video channel (www.YouTube.com/MrBuzzFactor).

I've also cranked out many more books, audio programs, and online courses, including two more books in this *Guerrilla Music Marketing* series, *Unleash the Artist Within*, *Killer Music Press Kits*, *Music Publicity Insider's Guide*, *How to Make Money as a DIY Musician*, *55 Ways to Promote & Sell Your Book on the Internet* – while also speaking at many music industry conferences.

Some nice perks have come my way as a result of this steadfast dedication to my topic. For instance, an earlier version of this book appeared in the major motion picture *The School of Rock*, starring Jack Black and Miranda Cosgrove. Berklee College of Music approached me to create an online course called "Music Marketing 101," which I also taught as an online faculty member.

I've been interviewed on NPR's "Morning Edition" and covered in *Electronic Musician, VIBE, American Songwriter, Music Connection, Canadian Musician*, and many other print and online publications.

Why the résumé listing? To make a point: I wasn't born into a wealthy family. I don't have friends who wield great power, nor do I have any special abilities. I'm certainly not a super salesman and I don't have a hyper, Type-A personality.

Insight: But I realized early on that I had a mind (just like you do) that I could use to make things happen. The only thing was, it seemed so many people around me felt as if they were victims of circumstance; that life handed them their fate and they were just along for the ride. That wasn't good enough for me.

After reading many inspiring books and pondering about life for a while, I came to the conclusion that our lives are simply a reflection of our accumulated thoughts and actions. There's a great quote by Earl Nightingale that goes, "We become what we think about most of the time." If you truly comprehend that simple statement, it will change your life.

The secret to musical success

The problem with people living dead-end lives is that they think dead-end thoughts. People who enjoy successful lives think successful thoughts – and then reinforce those thoughts with positive action.

Once I realized this simple but powerful truth, I started directing my thoughts in more productive ways. And the actions followed quite naturally. No doubt, I've stumbled many times on my journey through life and the music business (and I continue to), but the rewards have been many. And they keep growing every year.

Bottom line: *Thoughts are things.* What starts as an intangible concept grows into a reality as a result of mental focus combined with real-life activity. In fact, this is exactly how all songs are created.

So I ask you: What thoughts do you have about your present and future as an independent musician? And what actions are materializing as a result?

The *Guerrilla Music Marketing Handbook* will help you sort out the answers, open your mind to the infinite possibilities around you, and motivate you to take the steps necessary to climb higher up the ladder of success with your music.

How to use this book

Many of the chapters in this manual are written as stand-alone special reports. You can get a lot of value out of them without having to read previous chapters.

However, I do strongly suggest that you read the first two sections, "Guerrilla Music Basic Training" and "Guerrilla Music Marketing Online" from start to finish in their entirety. These chapters give you a great foundation for the information contained throughout the rest of the book. Other than that, feel free to examine the sections and chapters that relate to whatever marketing or music career topic you want to focus on at the time.

Warning: While I've gone to great lengths to load up this book with creative marketing tactics and techniques, I encourage you not to get so consumed by the tactical details that you lose sight of the big picture: making great music and sharing it with a growing number of fans. It's not the website, media exposure, or album cover art that's important. What's most essential is how those things help you connect with more fans in a meaningful way.

I'm grateful that you're allowing me to share these ideas with you. I sincerely hope you soak up the tips revealed in these pages and put them to good use. I look forward to one day hearing about your far-reaching musical achievements.

Much success to you. Now get out there and promote yourself!

-Bob

P.S. Remember to visit **worksheets.thebuzzfactor.com** to download the free Guerrilla Music Marketing worksheets that supplement this book, and go to **www.TheBuzzFactor.com** to get your free subscription to my Buzz Factor email newsletter.

Section 1:
Guerrilla Music
Basic Training

Chapter 1

3 Simple Steps to Effective Music Marketing

Ready to dive into this first chapter? Great. Here's a simple question for you:

What is music marketing?

Sure, you know it's something you have to do. You have at least some grasp of what is it. You recognize it when you see it (most of the time). But at its most basic level, can you explain what it is?

Do you really know what you are trying to accomplish when you get out there and start "marketing"? And more important, do you know WHY you engage in the promotional activities you choose to pursue?

Maybe you do. But then again, maybe you don't have a solid grasp of the underlying principles at work here.

So before we jump into building websites, seeking publicity, making sales offers, and other specific "tactics" of music marketing ... let's take a step back and examine why you're doing all of this stuff to begin with.

You see, many musicians (and creative people in general) are confused by this whole topic of marketing, self-promotion and sales. They think of it as a burden or a "necessary evil." So it's no wonder they struggle with it. After all, how many people will feel empowered by having to deal with a necessary evil?

Does this describe you?

Since you chose to read this book, you probably have a more friendly attitude toward marketing. Hopefully, you know that promoting yourself and your music is not a dastardly or manipulative deed at all. In fact, if you truly understand how your music positively affects your ideal fans, you quickly realize that introducing your music to new ears is an unselfish act of doing good in the world. And that's on the opposite end of the spectrum from "evil."

When I give workshops, I often ask, "How many of you feel uncomfortable about marketing and selling your music?" Usually 70% to 90% of the attendees raise a hand. Clearly, there's a lot of discomfort in this area.

Then I follow that up with another question: "How many of you are cool with the idea of sharing your music with people who are most likely to enjoy it?"

Almost every hand goes up. And it's no wonder. Most artists get a thrill out of hearing positive feedback from someone who has been exposed to their work. Therefore, creative people are generally comfortable with the idea of "sharing" their talents.

So, here's the first big revelation for you ...

Marketing is simply a strategic form of sharing!

And that's it.

If you're comfortable with the idea of sharing your music with people who will enjoy it, then you and I will have a great time as we work our way through the rest of this book.

Confusion sets in

Here's the thing: Even if you are content with the idea of strategic sharing (and I hope you are), it's a safe bet that you feel a void in your understanding of this immense subject. You may even feel confused, frustrated and overwhelmed by it. Can you relate?

Well, here's some news for you: *You are not alone!*

Everyone feels the confusion and bewilderment. Even I feel it at times – and I've been studying and teaching this topic for decades. So give yourself a break. You'll never know it all and do it all anyway. So relieve yourself of that burden now.

However, what you can do is ... *do what you can*. Do something, however small, every day. Chip away at your success. The more information you absorb, and the more you act on what you learn, the more clear you'll get about what you're doing and why you're doing it.

To help you get a jump-start on marketing clarity, I'm going to give you three simple principles to wrap your brain around. Think of them as a framework you can lay all of your music promotion and sales activities upon.

I'm a big fan of keeping things simple. Life is complicated enough as it is. We don't need to add complexity where it isn't needed.

I learned this valuable lesson years ago when trying to lose weight and get in better physical shape. I immersed myself in studying the best ways to live a healthy lifestyle. But guess what? The more I studied, the more confused I got. The more books I read, the more overwhelmed I felt.

There were so many formulas and methods to consider: The Atkins Diet, South Beach, Weight Watchers, the Zone – not to mention vegetarian, vegan and raw food options. On the fitness side, you could do aerobic exercise, strength training, yoga, spinning, Zumba, stair stepping, and more.

Then, one day I had a realization. I could take all the information I had consumed about health and fitness and summarize what I needed to do in four words:

Eat less. Move more.

That simplified the whole confusing process for me. If I stayed focused on those four words, I could make progress. And it made it easier for me to add more tactical activities to my life once I understood that basic framework. Then I could start making decisions about what I ate less of, and how I moved more, etc. But the basic premise underlying it all (*eat less, move more*) made it much easier to incorporate into my life.

So, let's start this exploration of music marketing with some similar basic principles.

The three stages of music marketing

I've been studying, researching, teaching, using, speaking and writing about music marketing for a good part of my life. I also practice what I preach and have successfully marketed my own music and books over the years. I've come to the conclusion that if you take all activities related to marketing, self-promotion and sales, they basically fall into one of three categories.

If you want to put this into simplistic "eat less, move more" terms, when it comes right down to it, music marketing consists of these three elements:

1) Creating awareness – taking action to communicate your musical identity to a specific audience

2) Building relationships – connecting, engaging, and interacting with a growing number of fans and media/business contacts

3) Generating revenue – asking for the sale and creating incentives for fans to spend money

There they are. The three stages of marketing. In a nutshell.

Seems simple enough, right? But the truth is, most self-promoting artists and music promoters get it wrong. They spend time on one or two of these stages but ignore the second or third. Or they get busy doing a bunch of marketing "stuff" but don't stop and think long enough to ponder how their efforts fit into this three-stage process.

My advice: *Please don't make these same mistakes!*

Want some examples?

Have you ever seen a band or record label run an ad that shouts out something along the lines of "*Wakeup Call*, the New Album From the ABC Band. Available

Everywhere!" All you get is the name of the band, the name of the album, and the fact that it is now on sale. Perhaps you've even created an ad or poster like this yourself.

What's wrong with this picture?

Well, with this promotion, the band is creating awareness, and it is asking for the sale. That's fine. But it leaves out an entire, all-important stage: developing relationships with fans.

This error would be especially unforgivable if this was the only marketing method the band was using. Why? Because consumers typically need repeated exposures to something before they'll get out their wallets. In addition, they need to feel a connection to the music and the artist. This ad does nothing to facilitate the relationship. It's simply an announcement. And that means wasted money spent on marketing.

Another example: Have you ever known (or been in) a wonderful band that does a great job of creating awareness and connecting with fans – perhaps through live shows? But then they drop the ball when it comes to asking for the sale and generating cash flow. They don't make people aware that they even have music for sale and don't make enticing offers for fans to buy now.

Again, they're only putting together pieces of the puzzle. And it's the missing pieces that stop them from truly making a difference and making money with their music.

The bottom line is, you must spend an equal amount of time and energy in all three areas to make progress. To help you better understand the three stages of music marketing, let's examine each one and go over a summary of things you can do in each area.

1) Creating awareness

This is the crucial first step. It's also the first thing that most people think of when they take action to promote themselves. These are the things you do to "get your name out there."

This is such an important step because you really can't do much with the next two stages until you're getting results from this one. Obviously, exposure is your main goal here. Before fans, the media, and other people in the music business can help you, they need to be aware of you. They need to be familiar with your name and the type of sound you create.

Here are some simple ways you can create awareness:

- Perform live as often as you can.

- Pin up posters to promote your live shows.

- Register a domain name and create an artist website.

- Set up profiles on the most prominent social media sites.

- Post music video clips on YouTube.com.

- Contact influential bloggers and podcasters.

- Pursue media coverage online and off.

- Write and distribute press releases.

- Pursue radio airplay online and off.

- Research and discover where your ideal fans congregate online and off.

- Determine the words and phrases that potential fans use to search for new music like yours.

- Optimize your web pages so they're more likely to be found with those keywords and phrases.

- Determine what popular artists you sound like and tie into those artists' existing fan bases.

This is just a quick overview of the steps involved in this stage (we'll get into more details about many of them later), but it should give you a good idea of what creating awareness is all about.

2) Building relationships

This is the step way too many aspiring (and impatient) musicians skip over. And they do so at their own peril. Quite often, artists don't even realize they're turning their backs on this step, or they don't comprehend the importance of it to begin with.

Core idea: As an independent artist, you can't think only in terms of marketing to the masses. That's an old-school, major-label strategy. So stop thinking about marketing as a way to catapult your message to an enormous, faceless crowd from a distance.

Guerrilla music marketing is personal. It's often delivered one-on-one. And even when you do direct a message to a sizeable audience, that audience is targeted and predisposed to like you. And, when communicating to crowds, your tone should be warm and personal. In fact, that's one of the things that sets you apart from bands that are mass-promoted and "handled" by corporations.

With this important, second stage of marketing, your goal is to move people along an ever-evolving path. Simply being aware of you is just the start. That awareness grows into enjoying your music, then to a greater familiarity and feeling an emotional connection with you. That feeling, among your strongest fans, is then transformed into a desire to support you and further enhance their lives with your music.

So, how do you start and maintain personal relationships with a growing number of fans and music business contacts? Here are just some of the actions you can take:

• Build a mailing list by collecting names and email addresses (and even cell phone numbers for text messages) at your live shows.

• Talk to people at your live events and become friends with your fans.

• Put an email sign-up form on every page of your website.

• Send email updates to your fan list once or twice a month.

• Mail postcard announcements to your fan list every once in a while.

• Communicate with editors, reviewers, bloggers, and podcasters in your genre and nurture relationships with them.

• Reply to all fan and industry emails promptly.

• Respond to people who post comments on your social media profiles to acknowledge that their efforts were noticed and appreciated.

• Start a blog and share your music-related thoughts and experiences – and encourage comments.

• Set up an online poll and ask fans to vote on your next album cover, T-shirt design, or set list.

• Thank your fans often and treat them well.

See how important this step is?

Your goal is not only to make people aware of you. Your goal is to notice the people who connect with you the most (or who can potentially help you the most) and nurture a bond with them repeatedly over time.

3) Generating revenue

Once you've created awareness and gotten on people's mental radars, and after you've engaged with your fans and built relationships with them, you are now ready for the third and final stage: making money.

I readily admit that this revenue-generating step is a tricky one that frustrates a lot of creative people. Some musicians are eager and ready to make money with their craft, while others are worried about being perceived as "greedy" or "hard sell" or "only in it for the money." There's so much emotional baggage concerning money, it's no wonder that countless artists are afraid to ask for the sale and encourage fans to spend money.

I get that. You're an artist first and a business person second. You value your integrity and don't want to tarnish your reputation with your fans.

Well, here's the good news: You can retain and honor your artistic integrity ... and still make good money with your music. It's not only possible, it is done every day by successful independent musicians around the world.

Reality: Do you want to know the biggest reason musicians have issues with earning an income from music? Insecurity. It's the feeling that their music has little value and is not worth paying for.

That's too bad. Because if they'd only take a few more steps to encourage fans to buy, these artists would find that fans have a different opinion. Most consumers who spend money on music feel that it enriches their lives. They have no problem parting with a small amount of cash to take home or download music that makes them feel good.

So get it into your head that your music is worth paying for. And make a commitment to this important third music marketing ingredient by doing the following things:

• Announce that you have CDs and merchandise for sale at your gigs – and have some fun with the ways you make these announcements.

• Set up an attractive, well-lit merchandise table at shows.

• Take a memorable line from one of your songs, print it on T-shirts, and sell them.

• Make your music available for sale on CD Baby, Amazon, and other prominent online music sales sites.

• Use a digital distribution service such as CD Baby or Tunecore to make your tracks available for sale on iTunes, Amazon MP3, and other major music download services.

• Stress fan benefits, not just the features of your music.

• Use testimonials from satisfied fans and the media.

• Offer a money-back guarantee on sales from your own website – yes, even for digital downloads.

• Sell more by offering a collection of your albums and merchandise at a special bulk price.

• Make limited-time and limited-quantity sales offers.

• Offer free bonuses to fans who buy now or at a minimum purchase amount.

• Sprinkle sales offers into your regular flow of social media updates.

Selling your music is not an evil or money-hungry deed. On the contrary, it's an essential element to serving your fans and building a successful music career.

As simple as one, two, three

Now you have the three steps to effective music marketing. I hope they help you get a firm grasp of the underlying principles beneath all promotion activities.

In addition, I hope you see how all three must work together. Awareness without a deeper relationship is fleeting. Trying to engage and interact with people who don't even know you exist is frustrating. Selling to an audience that doesn't feel a bond or sense of familiarity with you is futile.

So commit these three simple principles to memory. Engrave them in your brain. And the next time you create a new promotion plan, make sure your efforts are hitting on some combination of these three effective music marketing steps:

• **Creating awareness**

• **Building relationships**

• **Generating revenue**

Chapter 2

The Power of Goal Setting: A Foolproof Plan for Reaching Your Music Aspirations Faster

When the topic of goal setting comes up, most musicians run for cover. In fact, I'll bet that right now you're seriously thinking about skipping this chapter so you can move ahead to the "good stuff." That's understandable, but I urge you to ignore those instincts temporarily and stick with this page.

And while you're at it, relax. Planning for the future doesn't have to be painful. In fact, you'll find that getting on friendlier terms with the noble art of goal setting will propel you toward reaching your musical dreams – while also giving you more juice and energy to pursue them.

Of course, you may be one of those people who says, "Planning never gets me anywhere. I always run into brick walls and end up bitter and frustrated. No, I just like to let things happen and let nature take its course."

Don't lose control

While there's nothing wrong with letting your instincts guide you toward your true passion in life, taking the "let things happen" approach often leads to stagnation.

How else can you explain the large population of cynical, aimless musicians who populate most music scenes? They muddle through gig after gig (if they play out at all), waiting for nature to take its course, and then suddenly wake up one day and wonder why they're no better off today than they were 10 years ago.

The ugly truth: If you read nothing else in this chapter, at least contemplate this: When you just "let things happen" with your music career, you take the steering wheel of personal growth out of your hands. You'll always be at the mercy of someone or something else. In essence, you lose control over where you really want to take your skills and talents.

People who succeed in music use goal setting to get in the driver's seat and step on that accelerator pedal known as "accomplishment." (Pardon the poetic car analogies, but they help make the point.)

The good news is that you most likely already possess the skills to set goals effectively. Have you ever written a song? Have you ever gone into a studio to record your music? If so, you've been setting goals and didn't even realize it.

Question: When you showed up at the studio for your first recording session, what did you do? Did you look at your fellow band members and say, "Geez, I wonder what we should do now? Anybody got any good song ideas?"

Well, unfortunately, some musicians do this (and I think I've been in bands with some of them), but hopefully you realize that not being prepared is senseless. You've got money invested in the session, you've had a dream to put out your own album for years, plus you've got fans who are eagerly awaiting the recording ... you'd be nuts to go in there unprepared!

You didn't do that, did you?

Of course not. You went into that studio with a game plan – a list of songs, chord progressions, lyrics, knowing who's playing what parts and singing, when the harmonies come in, maybe even a title for the album. That's all that goal setting is: knowing what you want to do before you actually do it.

So in the same way you'd be wasting your time and money not being prepared to go into the studio, so too are you wasting your precious resources by being unprepared when it comes to your overall music career.

Does that make sense to you?

Being focused but flexible

Goal setting is not a rigid science. The plans you come up with are fluid – you can expect them to evolve and change over time. This is yet another concept you should be familiar with, especially if you're a songwriter. Many songwriters (myself included) write using just a guitar or piano and voice.

However, when many of these artists create a new composition, they often hear much more than that sparse arrangement in their heads. The drums, the bass part, maybe an entire string section ... all of it is there in the mind's ear. Perhaps you create the same way.

Then you take this skeleton of a song and share it with your other band members, explaining to each the parts you hear ringing through your gray matter. But the song the band ends up playing and recording is usually quite different from the version you originally heard in your head. However, the newer version is almost always better.

Bottom line: The plans you come up with when goal setting will change as you work toward them. But the mere act of coming up with an idea, visualizing it in your mind, and acting on it will drive you to take those first important steps. While the end result isn't always the one you expected, it's usually one you can learn and grow from and hopefully be proud of.

By pushing yourself, through advance planning, to head off in a specific direction – whatever direction that is – you create the opportunities from which real success can be realized. By waiting for things to happen, though, you set the stage for inaction and apathy. That's why setting goals for yourself and your music career is so important.

What follows are 11 helpful tips for getting the most out of goal setting:

1) Decide specifically what you want

Before you set out to conquer your music goals, you have to know what you really want. Do you have a clear idea of what you're going after? Sadly, when I ask musicians to tell me their goals, I often get answers such as "Book a lot more live shows" or "Sell a buttload of albums and music downloads."

Hmm … Let me ask you: Exactly how many is a "buttload"? How do you know when you have arrived at buttload status? And how much is "more"? The truth is, vague concepts about succeeding with music lead to vague, weak actions in attaining them.

The best goals are specific and measureable, such as "Book three live shows every month in Atlanta" or "Sell 100 physical CDs, 200 single downloads, and 50 album downloads by June 1." These goals are much more effective because they let you know right away if you reached them, exceeded them, or fell short. And when you effectively evaluate your results in this manner – which you should do often – the insight you gain will help you adjust your plan and your target.

So get crystal clear and detailed about what you want. The specific goals you identify will influence the focused actions you take, which will lead to increased results faster.

2) Visualize what you want as if you already have it

To add a lot more power to your goal setting, you should take the specific targets you identified in the previous step and create a clear picture of the outcome in your mind. Close your eyes for five to ten minutes every day and imagine what it will look like when you reach each goal. Immerse yourself in that picture and deeply feel the sensations. What would it look, sound, feel, taste and smell like if you were already in that enviable position? Use that vision to pull you toward it.

In 1977, when I was just 16 years old, I attended one of my first major concerts. The band was Led Zeppelin, featuring the original lineup. I was a huge fan and was thrilled beyond belief to experience the group live. I had been playing guitar for a couple of years at that point and, of course, idolized Zep guitarist Jimmy Page.

When I got home that night, I strapped on my electric guitar (unplugged so I didn't wake my mom) and played that Stratocaster like I never had before. I was emotionally energized as I saw myself onstage rockin' out to the masses. It was then that I set a goal to play music full-time within five years, by the time I turned 21. And I ended up doing just that. I believe the power of playing my guitar and mentally seeing myself onstage that night after the Led Zeppelin concert (and playing that same vision in my mind many times after) propelled me to reach that goal.

There's no doubt about it. Locking in mental images of your goals (combined with desire and emotion) will set you on an unstoppable course.

3) Write down your goals

Don't keep goals only in your head. Put ink to paper and commit them to a solid form. Writing down your goals adds another element of conviction to your intent to reach them. All of my accomplishments – publishing a music magazine, writing and publishing books, putting out independent music releases, leading workshops – started as notes to myself jotted down in a notebook. Don't overlook the power of the pen.

Yes, I know you can also capture goals and notes in electronic form, such as on your computer or mobile phone. And that's much better than having them float around in your brain. But I highly recommend you also write them out by hand. Doing so adds a physical aspect to your interaction with your goals, which helps ingrain them more fully into your being.

In fact, I encourage you to take this a step further and set aside at least 15 to 20 minutes every day to write your goals and ideas in a notebook. Use these sessions to brainstorm new ways to promote your music, find solutions to current problems, or craft lyrics to an original song. Whatever you do, spend time writing – then apply the things you've written to reach your goals.

Okay. You're doing great. See, this goal setting thing isn't so bad after all. We're on a roll, so let's keep going ...

4) Make a list of what's in it for you

Next, compile a list of ways you will benefit from achieving each goal. Of course, you instinctively know that you'll enjoy reaching your goals. But can you articulate exactly how and why you will benefit? Will you be rewarded with recognition, self-fulfillment, money, fame or creative satisfaction?

By listing these benefits in detail, you examine your true motivation for wanting each goal in the first place. You may discover the reasons that drive you aren't the most productive (such as being lured by the prospect of making lots of money, even though your heart isn't really into it). However, when you have a goal that's fueled by a genuine desire and true belief in your ability to attain it and enjoy the benefits, you'll be energized and ready to take on the challenges.

Another important thing to examine is how much you are pursuing these things for yourself vs. for the benefit of others. Most highly successful people come to the realization that lasting fulfillment always comes from providing value to other people (in your case, your fans) and enriching their lives. Make sure these aspects are among the reasons you desire your goals in the first place.

5) Anticipate the obstacles you'll encounter

Make no mistake about it, there will be bumps along the road to reaching your goals. You will encounter things that go wrong, people who disappoint you, and schedules that move much slower than you'd like. But don't let any of these obstacles stop you! Just try to anticipate some of the difficulties you might face, then plan for how effectively you'll deal with them when they arise.

Example: For five years I organized an annual music conference in the Midwest called the St. Louis Regional Music Showcase. It was an enormous undertaking, and every year I had to gather a team of volunteer organizers to help pull off the event. Without fail, every year one of my assigned organizers bailed out close to the event date, leaving that aspect of the conference in disarray.

It was frustrating, but it seemed to be the nature of the beast. Instead of getting too upset about it, I either found a replacement or ended up doing the job myself (not always an attractive option). But since I had mentally prepared myself for this possibility, I was able to find a way to work through it. Plan on doing the same thing along the road to reaching your goals.

Important: As with many things in life, balance is the key here. Don't obsess about things going wrong to the point it paralyzes you and keeps you from moving forward. On the other hand, don't anticipate a perfect outcome exclusively. That may set you up to be completely thrown off track when unexpected events occur. If there's one thing you can count on, it's your goals unfolding in a way you didn't plan. So find comfort in the imperfection of it all – then go for it!

6) Identify the people and resources you'll need

I admit, I'm a big proponent of the DIY (do it yourself) approach to life and work. For one, it suits my persona and general outlook regarding self-reliance as a way of life. Too many people look outside of themselves for answers first. When other people don't immediately step forward to help them, they feel like abandoned victims – which is not an empowering state to be in.

My philosophy: Your success starts from within. It's not something you go out there and "get." Success is a quality that first resides within you that you take with you wherever you go, regardless of what material circumstance suggest otherwise.

So, from my perspective, DIY is a foundational starting point and attitude that you operate from.

However, embracing DIY does not mean that you literally have to do it ALL yourself. To make progress and leave a legacy with your music, you absolutely must involve other people and resources. This includes your fans who will support you and the individuals and vehicles that will help you reach these fans. Now is the time to begin contemplating who and what they are.

So, start gathering information on the people, tools and information sources you may need to reach your goals faster. These might include live music venues, music websites, recording studios, music sales outlets, bloggers, podcasters, video production people, music conferences, booking agents, radio stations, magazines, graphic designers, producers, etc.

Compile this list of contacts from online searches, music business directories, and by networking with other musicians. Plus, you should always keep your eye open for new sources to add to the list – newspapers you pick up in other cities, music associations you read about, new resources you come across on the Internet, etc.

Your music career always starts with you. But to make progress, you must get involved with other people. Do you know who they are?

7) Set a deadline

Remember how you always got off your butt and went to work the night before a term paper was due at school? Deadlines have a way of motivating us to act. Commitments we make to ourselves and others can be powerful. Set a time limit for achieving each stage of your action plan ... then do whatever it takes to meet those deadlines.

Make sure your deadlines are realistic, though. If they're set too far in the future, there may be no motivation for you to get busy working toward them. If deadlines are set too soon, you risk encountering disappointment if you run out of time and miss them. So do your best to set sensible goals and deadlines.

While it's great to think long-term and consider where you want to be one year, three years, and even five years from now ... the sweet spot of detailed goal setting seems to be in the 90-day to six-month timeframe. So, by all means, set important milestones (like release a new album, go on a mini tour) in the more distant future. But concentrate most of your specific planning and effort on what you can accomplish in the next three months or so to move toward them.

8) Create your plan

After you've considered all of the previous steps, it's time to write the first draft of your action plan. To do this, start with a date that you would like to reach each goal and work backwards through the process. Break down every stage of the plan into its most basic tasks (such as doing research, making phone calls, sending email, designing websites and promotional materials, mailing packages, booking studio time, setting up meetings, writing songs).

Be sure to allow enough time for each stage. As you know, there will be unanticipated obstacles and distractions, so include breathing room in the plan to accommodate them. Then make a short list of the primary things that need to be done first – but make sure they're attainable beginning steps. For instance, if one of your goals is to perform at the Whisky a Go Go in Hollywood (and you have rarely played out before), calling the club would not be the first thing you'd do. There is a whole series of preliminary steps you'd need to take long before you ever got near the venue.

Another important distinction to make is knowing the difference between Projects and Next Action Steps. This is one of the profound takeaways I got from reading David Allen's book, *Getting Things Done*. A Project is a goal that requires multiple action steps (such as "Redesign the website"). A Next Action Step is the very first or next thing you can do to move forward on a Project.

Best practice: Make sure your daily to-do list consists only of Next Action Steps. If you include "Redesign the website" or "Promote the next show" on your list of things to do today, you will likely feel overwhelmed by the immensity of it. Compare that to a list that includes specific actions such as "Email Phil to get the name and number of the web designer he recommended" or "Create a Facebook event page for the May 17 gig." Those are much more specific, attainable tasks you can act on.

The key to creating goal-setting plans that work is being laser-focused on the very next thing that needs to be done to make progress. Got it? Great. Now get to work and write that first-draft plan!

9) Clear your mind, then re-examine your plan

Now get away from your plan for a day or so and let the details float around in your subconscious mind while you work on other things. (Note: This is one of the few times I'll suggest you *not* take immediate action.)

After some time away, come back to the plan with a fresh eye and evaluate the logic in your sequence of events. For instance, have you really allowed enough time for the recording of your demo? Or perhaps you're being too easy on yourself by allowing six months to get your first band photo taken. (I've known bands that have been together for years and never had a promotional photo taken. In fact, I think I was in one.)

More questions: Are you juggling too many or too few projects at the same time? Also ask yourself what additional help you might need with technical support, media contacts, artwork, web design, press releases, and more. Also, let a few people you trust look over your plan and ask for their feedback. Better yet, read the plan to them out loud. Hearing yourself verbalize your goals can reveal strengths and weaknesses you wouldn't become aware of otherwise.

Next, using your newfound insights, create a second-draft plan as best you can. But remember, it doesn't have to be perfect to use. Don't fool yourself into thinking you can't get started just because there are a few details you don't know yet. Trust your abilities and know you'll handle whatever needs to be done when demanding situations arise.

Which leads to ...

10) Act on your goals now!

At some point (sooner rather than later) you must get busy working on the plan you've just created. It's sad, but a lot of great ideas have withered away because the person who came up with them never took action. Don't let this be your fate. Don't wait for nature to take its mystical course.

Vow that every day you will take some action based on your goal-setting plan. Even if you think you don't have time or aren't feeling motivated, do at least some small deed every single day. Even if it's simply making one phone call to a media contact, sending one press kit to a venue owner, leaving a comment on a blog or social media site, sending one email update to your fan list ... do something every day!

At the beginning of every week, take a look at the high-priority projects you want to make progress on over the next one to six months. For each project, make a list of the small, Next Action Steps you can take this week. Every day you should look at this list, pick something from it, and DO IT! And do it NOW!

That's how successful musicians get things done, create a body of creative output, build a career, and leave a legacy. You can do the same thing – if you are willing to take action every day.

11) Measure your progress and make adjustments

Once you have been working on your plan for a few weeks to a couple of months, you must then determine if your actions are leading you in the right direction. Are you moving closer to your goals or further away? Is your progress happening slower or faster than you had hoped?

The only way to answer these questions is to regularly evaluate your plan and measure your progress. That's why it's so important to have specific goals with numbers and deadlines attached to them (see tips #1 and #7 earlier in this chapter). If you find that you're way behind schedule on getting things done, ask yourself what you can do to get the results you really want. Don't just get frustrated and give up. Making adjustments to your plan is an essential part of any goal-setting process.

So be prepared to measure often. Then celebrate your wins and come up with solutions to shortfalls.

Key point: When something is working, fit more of it into the plan. When other aspects prove to be duds (like the drummer's bright idea to send your guitar player to local radio stations dressed like a gorilla), cut back or drop them completely. Fine-tuning is what crafting an effective goal-setting plan is all about.

Don't forget, you can download free worksheets that go with this chapter and the others in this book. Just head to **worksheets.thebuzzfactor.com** to grab them.

Now you have the 11 key elements of setting goals that will help you reach your music aspirations faster. Use them to focus your energy and give yourself an immense boost toward getting what you really want from your music – and from your life!

Chapter 3

The First 5 Steps to Marketing (and Profiting From) Your Music

I get it. I feel your pain.

I'm not talking about physical pain, of course. I'm referring to the emotional pain and frustration that come with pouring your heart into your band, recording project, live show, or other music-related pursuit ... and still feeling like you're coming up short.

Whether you produce pop, rock, jazz, hip-hop or baroque speed metal bluegrass, you know what you offer is good and is of value to others. It's just that not enough people seem to know about you yet. And, as a result, not nearly enough money is streaming in to cover expenses, much less give yourself a little take-home money.

Take heed, my fellow Guerrilla Music Marketer. This chapter sheds light on how to remedy your situation (without losing your sanity or forcing you to start a Justin Bieber tribute band). What follows are five steps you must follow to take charge of your music marketing so you start profiting from it now!

Warning: Don't make the mistake that many aspiring musicians will make. They'll read these steps, tell themselves how valuable the advice is, and then go right back to the same destructive routines as before. Please don't do that.

To help you develop new and empowering habits, I've added an affirming commitment statement to the end of each step. Read them out loud every day for two or three weeks until each commitment becomes ingrained. Then read them at least once a week after that. Doing so will make certain you put these success tips into action ... and profit accordingly.

1) Have a clear idea who your ideal fan is

Could you sit down right now and write a profile of your ideal fan? How old are they? Do they tend to be male or female? Can you articulate how your fans dress, where they work, what TV shows they watch, which blogs they read, what they do for fun, and who their favorite cultural hero is?

If you can't describe your fans in detail, you should immediately start searching for a way to do so. Knowing precisely who your fans are dictates what avenues you use to reach them and how you communicate your message once you do reach them.

Reality: Continuing to ignore these insights will lead to missed opportunities and wasted time. If you don't know where your fans hang out, what they're interested in, and why they spend money, how will you ever be able to effectively promote your talents in a way that will lead to all of you being better off?

When you overlook this element, potential fans move on without the benefit of your music. And you stumble on without the satisfaction of having shared your music and getting the recognition and financial rewards that come with it. Believe me, knowing who your fans are makes marketing your music a lot easier.

The solution: Do some basic, informal research. If you perform live at all, start asking questions of people in the crowd during breaks and after your shows. What types of people come to see you? What traits do your fans have in common? Write down your observations.

You can also reach out to your existing fans or a group of friends you trust by email and simply ask them to reply to a few questions about who they are, what they do, how they discover new music, etc. There are also a number of free services that allow you to conduct online polls. Put these tools to good use.

However you do it, get busy gathering this important information. Doing so may even allow you to discover a segment of the population you've been ignoring but could benefit from your music.

If you're just starting out, observe the types of people who patronize similar artists. Or simply describe the type of person to whom you want your band or record label to appeal. If you're still stumped on figuring out who your fans are, here's an effective trick: Look in the mirror. That's right, the best indicator of who your fans are is you! If you created the music, it's a natural extension of you. Therefore, people just like you should be attracted to it.

So ... where do *you* hang out online and off? How do *you* discover new music? What types of websites and entertainment channels do *you* frequent? There's a good chance your ideal fans are doing the same thing.

This doesn't have to be a complicated research project. Just get a handle on the types of people you want to reach with your promotional and sales messages. Doing so will help you get to them faster.

Affirm your commitment to step 1:

"I no longer leave my music marketing to chance. Through basic research, personal observation and gut instincts, I create a specific profile of my ideal fan. Using this profile, I know who my ideal fans are and how to reach them effectively."

2) Discover what motivates your fans

Now that you have a clearer idea of who your fans are, you have to reach out and touch them. But the only way to reach them effectively is to understand their real reasons for spending time and money on you.

The problem: Most music marketers concentrate on themselves and the features of their product or service. For instance, recording studios are notorious for promoting lists of equipment and the credentials of engineers. That's not a crime, but the real reason most studio clients spend money is to get the good feeling of hearing a professional-sounding recording of their music (because of the equipment). They may also crave the anticipated respect they'll get from being closely associated with a prominent person in the music industry (due to the engineer's résumé).

While the studio literature and sales pitch should be stressing the clients' feelings of accomplishment and respect, they instead spit out a list of mechanical features. Your real goal with marketing and sales is to push a consumer's hot buttons – the deeper reasons he or she spends time and hard-earned money on a given product or service.

Keep in mind that every one of your fans (and every human being on the planet, for that matter) is tuned into radio station WII-FM. Those call letters stand for "What's In It For Me?" It's the essential question that every person asks when confronted with a time or money decision.

How will you answer that question?

If all you do is talk about your credentials, your music, and yourself ... most people will tune out and move on to something else. And they'll quickly forget about you. But if you start off by letting your potential fans know how they can benefit from your music, then you'll get their attention. And once you've got their attention, you'll have a few more precious seconds to occupy a space in their brains. So don't squander that opportunity.

Do you know how fans benefit from your music? Can you articulate how your music will make them feel? Think about it. Does your music pump them up, chill them out, or put them in a mood to get down on the dance floor? Do your lyrics make them think, smile, laugh, or cry? How does your music help them reinforce an idea they already have of themselves? Think like a fan instead of like a musician and really give this some thought.

More questions: Does your music make listeners feel good? If so, in what way? Does it give them a recreational escape from their worries? Does it allow them to hang onto something they're afraid of losing, such as youth, sex appeal, or an outlet for their frustrations? Your goal is to determine the real motivating feeling – the key benefit – that people experience when they spend time and money on you.

Ask your fans more questions, make more observations, do your homework, and use your head. Discovering the key motivations that draw your fans to you will help you discover your road to success in the music business.

Affirm your commitment to step 2:

"I have a sincere interest in knowing how and why my fans enjoy my music. I now do whatever it takes to uncover the personal and emotional benefits that motivate people to spend time and money on my music. Discovering these hot buttons allows me to more effectively market the music I have to share with the world."

3) Create and use a Brand Identity Statement (BIS)

Think of your band or music business as the steel tip of a dart. Now visualize that the people of the world are spread out across a giant wall filled with thousands of dartboards. Each dartboard represents a specific group of people. For instance, one might be teenagers who like hard rock music while another symbolizes adults who enjoy the blues. Other dartboards might include fans of folk, bluegrass, acid jazz, punk, smooth R&B, and so on.

Key: When you market your music, it's your job to aim the tip of your dart directly at the bull's-eye of the dartboards that represent your ideal fans. You do this by sending targeted messages to the websites, blogs, podcasts, online forums, newspapers, magazines, and radio stations that your potential fans visit, read and consume.

That's the whole point of all this marketing research. Once you know who your ideal fans are, you can determine what forms of media they patronize. You then send focused messages through these channels.

But what kind of messages do you send? Most people who market independent music make one of two mistakes. They either:

     1) Throw their dart randomly all over the wall and end up reaching no one who is interested in what they do, or ...

     2) Aim their dart at the proper boards, but the message is so vague or confusing, the dart doesn't stick to any of them

The solution: Create a Brand Identity Statement (BIS) about your music. A BIS is a simple but powerful sentence of no more than 15 words (10 words or less is even better) that describes the specific vision of your songs, image, band or record label. If you could take every feature and beneficial aspect associated with your music and run them through a grinder, only to be left with the pure, concentrated essence of you and your music ... that would be your BIS.

You should craft your BIS to include a benefit statement to your fans. Two well-known Brand Identity Statements from the traditional business world are Domino's

"Fresh, hot pizza delivered to your door in 30 minutes or less, guaranteed" (13 words) and M&M's "Melts in your mouth, not in your hands" (eight words).

The BIS I use to promote my TheBuzzFactor.com website is "Music marketing tips and self-promotion ideas for independent songwriters, musicians and bands." For my Artist Empowerment Radio podcast, I use "Self-promotion tips and inspiration for musicians, artists, writers and creative people of all kinds."

Examples: Here are a few possible Brand Identity Statements for bands:

- "Old-school funk for people who like to dance"

- "Frank Zappa meets Frank Sinatra at a rodeo"

- "Erotic techno grooves for sensuous souls"

Other BISs might include the following:

- A recording studio could use "High-quality demos for bands on a budget."

- A solo artist targeting bar owners might use "Riveting acoustic folk music to help you sell more beer."

- A small ticket agency's BIS could be "Convenient access to the great shows the big promoters miss."

You can use your Brand Identity Statement in two ways. One is internal; the other external.

Internal – Having a BIS keeps you focused on your marketing message. Therefore, every time you write a press release, set up a photo session, do a radio interview, or design an album cover, you make certain your vision stays focused on your core identity. You wouldn't want your album cover to convey humor while the faces in your band photo look grim and serious.

Also, using a BIS keeps your marketing message tight and consistent. You don't want to send out a press release about your band's new online resource for ska fans, then do a radio interview and end up talking only about the night you met Pat Sajak. By constantly referring to your BIS, you make sure the messages you send stay focused on the most potent aspects of your music.

External – You can also use your BIS as a public slogan that appears on all of your web pages, fliers, banners, posters, T-shirts, stickers, and more. That way, whenever people hear your name, they will be reminded of your musical identity and what's in it for them.

Here are some real-life examples of other Brand Identity Statements in use:

• The band Buck O Nine describes its music as "Rock-steady ska-core from southern California."

• H&B catalog of Jazz CDs claims to be "A mail order service for people who know jazz."

• Chicago's Smart Studios promotes itself with "Great sounds. Cool people. Killer studio."

Find your own BIS. Then use it to stay focused and hammer home your primary marketing message to the masses.

Affirm your commitment to step 3:

"I will never again 'wing it' when it comes to marketing my music. I now use a powerful Brand Identity Statement to promote my music. I use my BIS to develop a consistent, needle-sharp vision and focused public image of my unique niche in the world of music."

4) Focus on the benefits your music delivers

Now it's time to connect with the music fans whose lives you are about to touch and improve. But first we're going to dissect the way you communicate with these fans. Let's start by using the information you gathered about who your fans are and why they spend time and money on you. Then you'll use those details as you pursue various means of communicating your message, including:

• Press releases sent to the media

• Business cards and postcards

• Your electronic press kit and photos

• Your website and web pages

• Social media profiles online

• Blogs

• Podcasts

• Music video clips

• Email messages

• Voice mail

- Posters and fliers

- Radio interviews

- Album cover artwork

- Paid ads

Bottom line: As you create the marketing materials listed above, you must keep one thing foremost in mind: the needs of your fans! In other words, stop talking so much about yourself, your needs, and your qualifications. Start talking about what matters most: The benefits fans get when they support, consume and purchase your music.

"The objective here is plain," says marketing expert Jeffrey Lant. "It is not merely to tell what you've got ... it's to motivate a human being to take immediate action so you can move to the next stage of the marketing process."

In his book *No More Cold Calls*, Lant advises, "You must list every feature of your service, transform every one into a benefit, then make sure the benefit is as specific and enticing as possible."

Let's see how this works in the real world. As an example, I'll use the way I've marketed some of my downloadable, spoken-word audio programs. I'll list each feature first, then its corresponding benefit.

Feature: Sixty minutes in length.

Benefit: Jammed packed with a full hour of music career-boosting details you can start using the same day you order.

Feature: Available only in audio format.

Benefit: Soak up these useful success secrets at your convenience: while you drive, jog, ride a bike, or clean the house. Audio books make learning easy.

Feature: It's an MP3 download.

Benefit: Why wait? Start putting these ideas to use immediately. Get instant access as soon as your order is approved online.

Here are a couple of ways you might apply this principle to a new music release:

Feature: Mastered by a Grammy Award-winning producer.

Benefit: You'll experience crystal clear sound that will transport you to another dimension.

Feature: We were voted Best Rock Band in Detroit.

Benefit: Don't miss out. Join the party and find out what thousands of Detroit rock fans are raving about.

Get the idea? You must learn to always do this when describing your music.

Affirm your commitment to step 4:

"No more bland feature listings for me! I now take every aspect related to my music and identity and transform them into benefits that my clearly defined audience of potential fans finds irresistible."

5) Stop talking so much about yourself

I know it seems like we've beaten this premise to death. But just in case it hasn't sunk in, let's drive it home one more time: Make certain your words – whether in person or on the phone, by email or on your website, in ads or on postcards – focus on the benefits to your fans.

Time and time again I explained this essential concept to the business owners who advertised in my former music newspaper. And, sure enough, when they turned in the wording for their ads, they were filled with "I do this, we've done that, I, me, mine ... blah, blah, blah!"

Reality: Human beings gravitate toward talking and thinking about themselves – and for a good reason. For millions of years, members of our species had to think about their own needs to survive. In the caveman days, if you weren't consumed with self-preservation, you'd be consumed by any number of wild predators, not to mention being done in by members of rival tribes. There's a long-standing tradition of human self-indulgence.

So you're not going to wipe out millions of years of conditioning in a couple of days. But you can use your advanced, reasoning brain to resist these primitive urges when it comes to marketing your music-related pursuits.

Also, realize that you can use this knowledge of human nature to your advantage. When you communicate with potential fans through your live shows, website, business cards, press kits and so on, who will these fans be focusing on? Don't kid yourself and think it's you.

Knowing this, give fans what they want and make sure your marketing message hits them squarely on the head with what's in it for them. Lead off with the number one benefit fans get from you, followed by the number two benefit, and so on. Pile the motivating reasons they should care about you one on top of the other until even the most thickheaded of humans can figure it out.

A more specific example: Let's say you were put in charge of marketing a new electric drill for homeowners. How would you go about it? Most people would start listing features: the manufacturer, mechanical specs, and material the drill is made of … all focusing on (you guessed it) the drill.

But what do people really want when they buy a drill?

A hole.

They also want a hole that can be created quickly, easily and economically. It doesn't matter if the hole gets there because of a drill, a toaster, a pair of socks, or a monk – as long as the appropriate hole is conveniently created in the appropriate place.

In other words, sell the hole, not the drill. Then, and only then, use your features to show how your drill can meet the customer's specific needs.

Affirm your commitment to step 5:

"It isn't all about me. I resist the human urge to talk about myself and will, instead, focus on what my fans are most interested in: what's in it for them!"

There you have it: The first five steps to more effective music marketing. Now affirm your commitment to these principles and get busy thinking, observing, asking questions, researching your ideal fans, creating a BIS, and focusing on the benefits you offer. A world of notoriety and profit awaits you.

Chapter 4

The #1 Question You Must Answer When Promoting Your Music

I'm going to use this entire chapter to deal with only one subject because it's so vital to the success of your music promotion efforts. Every day I see the same mistake being made in this area and feel I owe it to you to drive home this crucial point.

Imagine you walked into a retail store that sells music, and one of the employees (a complete stranger to you) came up and handed you a box filled with CDs. Then he said, "Here, these are promo copies we're giving away. You can have any CD you want out of the box. But you can take only one."

Now let's pretend that you were not familiar with any of these artists. As you looked at each CD to consider whether or not you wanted it, what would be the first question to pop into your head? In other words, what basic question would you need to answer first before you could make an intelligent (and quick) decision on which one you'd take?

Would it be "Who produced this album?"

No.

Would it be "What record label put this out?"

Probably not.

How about "Where is this act from?" or "How many awards has this band won?"

No. And no.

Would it be "How highly do these musicians think of their own music?"

No.

Hopefully, you've come to the same conclusion that I have. The first question that anyone asks when encountering new music is ...

What kind of music is this?

I use this box of free CDs example to make a point: This is exactly the same position that music editors, bloggers, podcasters, booking agents, program directors, A&R people, and music publishers are in when they receive your unsolicited recordings along with dozens of others. This is also what potential fans experience when they encounter you for the first time.

Even though it's great to think that everyone already knows who you are and what you do, the sad truth is that most people you contact will be clueless. That's why giving them the first and most important clue up front is essential.

Key point: Human beings need some way to process information and file it away in the proper place in their heads before moving on to any follow-up questions, such as "Where is this band from?" or "What unique spin do they put on this genre?"

Without creating a mental category or comparison to something that each person is already familiar with, it's nearly impossible to get to these important follow-up questions. And if you can't move this sorting-out process along in a swift manner, your music marketing efforts end up dead in the water.

Why, then, do so many people who promote music either ignore answering this fundamental question – *What kind of music is this?"* – or bury the answer so deep in their promotion materials that the reader gives up out of frustration before ever uncovering it?

Unless you are (or are working with) a well-known artist, the people receiving your promo kits and marketing messages will be in the dark regarding who you are and what you play. Your job, therefore, is to answer that first all-important question right off the bat: "What kind of music is this?" It should be one of the first things people see when viewing your press kit, website, or any other marketing tool you create.

Straight from the slush pile

Here's an example I pulled out of an overflowing box of review CDs years ago when I was a music editor. After opening the package, the first thing I see is a cover letter. Here's how it reads (I've changed the name of the person, record label and band to protect the misguided):

"My name is John Jones, vice president of Widget Records, here in New York. I'm writing to announce that one of our bands, the Losers, will be playing in St. Louis on July 24."

It's important to Jones that he announces who he is and what he does right off the bat. I'm sure this makes him feel good about himself. But how does this introduction move him closer to his goal of getting media coverage for the poor Losers? At least I know about the St. Louis date, something that should matter to me. But since I don't know what kind of music this is, I'm not impressed.

On to the next paragraph ...

"The Losers' music is already on national college and commercial radio."

Excellent. His mother must be very proud. But is this jazz radio? Alternative radio? Polka radio? Ten stations? Eight hundred stations? What? I'm still being kept in the dark.

"The Losers are a new band founded in New York City. These shows are part of a year-long tour to promote their debut album."

More senseless background details before I even know what kind of music this band plays. But one thing I do know is that Jones sure likes talking about his band and its accomplishments. Now I'm starting to doze off.

A musical diamond in the rough

So I keep reading anyway, and finally, I come across this gem:

"The Losers' music combines Celtic violin with punk-influenced distorted guitars and melodic rock vocals ..."

What? A description of the music? Say it isn't so! And I only had to wait till the fourth paragraph to get it. And it ends up being a pretty cool description: Celtic violin with punk guitars. Now that's different. That's something I'd like to take a quick listen to. What a great media hook for the band!

Unfortunately, the label's vice president has done the group a disservice by burying this vital piece of information in a dreary cover letter. Most media people would have given up on it long before they got to the intriguing description.

But this never occurred to Jones. It was much more important for him to pound his chest and proclaim his name, title, city, and the fact that his as-yet-undefined band was getting radio airplay. What a missed opportunity! Don't make this same error.

There's a better way

How much more effective would Jones have been if his letter went something like this?

Dear Bob,

When we first told people we had signed a band that combined Celtic violins with distorted punk guitars and melodic rock vocals, they told us we were crazy. But we proved them all wrong with the Losers, a band that is now on a major roll. Last month alone, more than 325 college stations around the country were playing cuts off the band's new self-titled CD.

And now you can experience the Losers yourself when they come to St. Louis on July 24. I think your readers would get a kick out of hearing about this unusual Celtic/violin/punk-rock mix.

Admit it. This version pulls you in and lets you know what you're dealing with quickly and interestingly – as opposed to the dry meanderings of the original cover letter.

Are you guilty of a PR felony?

Take a look at the promotional tools you're using now. What's the first thing you see? Your address? The band members' names? The record label name? Some vague reference to how impressive your music is without a specific definition of it?

Stop beating around the bush and start getting to the heart of the matter. Media and industry people are overworked and distracted. Fans are bombarded with information overload. Don't shroud your message in mystery, hoping it will tease people and make them read further.

Remember this: No one will ever be as interested in reading your marketing materials as you are.

So give them what they need up front, fast and simple. And answer the most important question first:

"What kind of music is this?"

Now that you have a solid grasp of the foundational elements of guerrilla music marketing, it's time to expand your horizons. In the next section we delve into the great digital frontier and how to make good use of all the Internet has to offer talented musicians like you!

Section 2:
Guerrilla Music Marketing Online

Chapter 5

Five Principles of Internet Marketing Every Musician Should Know

Billions of people around the planet now have access to the Internet. That's a lot of people and a lot of opportunities at your fingertips. It can also be bewildering, as the number of new music sites and the variety of online tools continue to grow at dizzying rates. Just when you get a handle on how to promote yourself effectively with all of the existing web-based tools, a dozen new ones come along to cloud your vision and fill up your to-do list.

Here's something I recommend you do this very moment: *Take a deep breath*.

Relax. Relieve yourself of the burden to know it all and do it all. Because, guess what? You never will know it all and do it all anyway – so don't set yourself up for guaranteed frustration by setting unrealistic expectations, especially when it comes to using digital technology.

The good news: While you will never know everything there is to know about online music promotion, and you'll never get around to doing all that needs to be done, you can indeed get a better understanding of what the Internet and digital tools are. Once you understand these basic principles it will be a lot easier to implement an action plan and expand your efforts.

The rest of this chapter will be devoted to giving you a quick crash course on the five most important things you need to know about marketing your music on the Internet today.

1) Understand the long tail of abundance

There's a good chance you may have run across references to "the long tail" in your search for marketing advice. It's a term made popular by Chris Anderson, who wrote a book some years ago called *The Long Tail: Why the Future of Business Is Selling Less of More*. Addressing this topic is a great way to ease into a better understanding of how to think about marketing in this modern era.

The Long Tail was a real eye-opener for me, because in the book Anderson writes at length about the changing face of the entertainment industries. Here's a summary of the concept, with my own spin on it:

For decades, we lived in a scarcity economy. We got introduced to new music, books and films via traditional sources such as retail outlets, radio stations, television programs, and print publications. But all of these avenues of exposure had physical limitations. There was only so much shelf space, air time and editorial pages to fill. So, in order to appeal to the widest audience and turn a profit, only those things that were determined to be the most popular (and therefore most profitable) were stocked or covered.

Insight: This lead to a lopsided cultural mentality: A book, band or movie was either a big hit or a giant dud. There was little ground in between the two extremes of popularity. You were either part of the corporate media machine ... or an "underground" outsider.

Then came the growth and popularity of online retailers such as Amazon and Netflix, which were not constrained by the physical space limitations of traditional sellers.

For example, the biggest physical bookstores carry about 150,000 titles, while Amazon offers more than 10 million books. The average video rental store carries about 3,000 DVDs, while Netflix offers close to 100,000. The average Wal-Mart store carries less than 5,000 music CDs (filled with close to 60,000 individual tracks), while the iTunes music store offers more than 20 million individual tracks.

As you can see, with virtually unlimited digital shelf space, practically everything that is published can be made available for sale online. But here's where things get even more interesting ...

According to *The Long Tail* book and other sources, about 25% of the total revenues on Amazon and other online sellers come from products not available in retail stores. On the streaming music service Rhapsody, that usage figure is about 40%.

Yes, consumers are buying and getting exposure to many titles that are outside the traditional "hit list." Anderson's research concluded that, when given unlimited choice (along with the ability to filter through the choices), people will stray from the hits and spend a considerable amount of money on non-mainstream products.

Good news and bad

This is great news for independent musicians, because that means it is quite possible to reach the public as an artist not supported by a corporate entity. Unfortunately, the old scarcity business model is so ingrained in our culture, it has lead to many unfounded beliefs, such as:

- If it isn't a hit, it's a miss

- The only success is mass success

- "Independent" = "They couldn't get a deal"

- Low-selling = low-quality

- If it were good, it would be popular

Luckily, a growing number of creative entrepreneurs are figuring out ways to shatter these old notions and make the most of this new "abundance economy" – where practically everything is available to the public, where the cream rises to the top based on what consumers actually want, and where you can make an impact (and a living) without ever ranking on the Billboard Hot 100 list.

So, what kind of world do you want to live in? One of scarcity, hits and misses? Or one of abundance, hits and niches? The choice is ultimately up to you.

2) Embrace the age of the empowered music fan

Another big change the Internet has brought involves the evolution of the tech-savvy, modern music consumer. This is crucial to your future success with music, so read carefully:

Old-school music business: Back in the day, record labels would determine who the ideal audience was for a given act. Then they would hunt down those specific types of fans via targeted radio stations, magazines, concert venues, retail outlets, etc.

As I mentioned earlier, music consumers had limited ways of gaining access to new music, so they relied on commercial, programmed media sources to deliver new artists to them. Sure, some adventurous fans made the extra effort to find new music via "alternative" sources such as fanzines, college radio stations, mix tapes, etc. But most people weren't willing to work that hard to discover fresh sounds.

So music consumers were mostly *prey* – reactive to the efforts major labels made to track them down and feed them the latest music. That's where the term "target marketing" comes from. You aim your marketing message at your prey and fire away.

New-school music landscape: Today music fans are in control. They rely less and less on programmed, spoon-fed media sources and are finding it easier than ever to discover new music on their own. Using smartphones, tablets, digital music players, satellite radio, MP3 downloads, streaming music services, podcasts, digital video recorders, and more ... consumers now determine what they want to hear, when they want to hear it, and how.

The hunted become the hunters

Consumers who in the past were primarily hunted down by the music industry have now become proactive hunters, empowered to seek out and choose the music that's best suited for them. This shift has thrown the creation, promotion and distribution of music into a tailspin.

That's one of the biggest concepts I've been stressing lately. For years I've talked about "artist empowerment" and how musicians should take their careers into their own hands. That idea is true now more than ever. But what needs to be equally stressed is the huge shift toward "music fan empowerment" and "consumer empowerment."

Insight: For a long time now I've repeated the mantra that "we live in an incredible era of self-expression and self-empowerment." But these opportunities don't exist only for artists. They're available to everyone.

And that's why social sharing sites, blogs, podcasts, and online video are so popular. They give average people a chance to express themselves, connect with other people, and discover cool new things.

3) Get into the discovery zone

Consumers today don't respond very well to being "marketing to" in the traditional ways. However, they are more passionate than ever about discovering new music. It's just that now they prefer to discover it on their own or through a recommendation from a friend or trusted blogger, podcaster, music magazine, etc.

As an indie artist, what should you do in this environment?

You should still understand who your ideal fan is and actively seek them out. Simultaneously, you need to put yourself in the best position to be "discovered" – not by a record label A&R rep, but by a curious music fan in search of his or her new favorite song or artist.

Weird example: In some of my live workshops I ask attendees to imagine the following scenario: It's a bright, sunny day and you are on a float trip with friends on a calm, flowing river. Visualize yourself drifting along comfortably on an inner tube. There are small groups of people doing the same thing ahead of you and behind you on the river. You feel relaxed and content as you float on the water.

All of a sudden you hear someone screaming around the next turn in the river. As you get closer you see a guy standing on the bank holding a blue bowling ball under one arm. His other arm is waving as he shouts, "Hey! Check this out! I just made a cool new bowling ball. It's awesome! You should buy one now! Come on, man!"

What's wrong with this scenario?

Of course, it's awkward. It's also distracting, annoying and completely out of place. The sad thing is, this is exactly the way a lot of musicians promote themselves. They think they need to scream louder than everyone else and interrupt people to get their attention.

I have to give them credit for at least doing something to promote their music. They're doing the best they can. But they're going about it all wrong!

There's a better way: Forget about the guy with the bowling ball and go back to visualizing that lazy day floating down the river. Now imagine the bright sunlight is starting to take its toll on your eyes as you squint to look at the natural beauty around you.

You say to your friends floating nearby, "I forgot my sunglasses in the car. Does anyone have an extra pair?" Sadly, none of your friends can help you. Then you hear a voice from a short distant down the river.

"Hey, I've got an extra pair," says a woman you've never met before. "I don't need them back. They're yours – my gift to you."

She paddles toward you and hands you a pair of nice-looking shades. You put them on and they fit perfectly. "Thanks," you say, "these are awesome."

Your new friend replies, "My pleasure. Squinting can be a real pain. I'll tell you what, my car is parked about a half a mile down the river, and I've got a whole trunk full of glasses like these in different colors and styles. If you want, I'd be happy to show them to you. And anything you want to buy I can give you at half off the normal price."

Question: What's different about this interaction?

While this might still seem like an odd example, I hope you agree that this second scenario is a lot more appropriate and comfortable. Mostly important, the addition of the new person into the scene is relevant. No screaming or interrupting was necessary.

You were in need of something specific, and someone showed up at the right time to deliver it in a helpful manner. And they actually gave you a free sample of the thing you wanted and made sure you liked it before suggesting a financial transaction.

How does this all relate to Internet marketing?

You need to create a presence online in the many places where your ideal fans are naturally hanging out. That's why you should be set up on Facebook, Twitter and YouTube. That's why you should publish video content and maybe even a blog or a podcast. That's why you need to be actively encouraging and participating in relevant conversations online.

Put yourself in a position to be discovered by fans in a way that has you showing up as a perk and not a pest!

4) Tap into the filters your fans use

In the old scarcity economy model, the music that got stocked in stores, played on the air, and covered in the press was determined by what Chris Anderson calls "pre-filters." They included record label executives, retail store buyers, radio and TV program directors, magazine editors, etc. They were the "gatekeepers" of the traditional music business.

Actually, these pre-filters are still very much a force to this day but, as I'll show in a moment, their power is dwindling. So it's this small elite group that decides what is worthy of entering the corporate pipeline. Their decisions are made in two ways:

• They stock, broadcast and cover more of what has already proven itself popular, giving the general public more of what it seems to want.

• Of the new artists and albums that come out every month, the pre-filters predict what they think will be popular (in addition to giving prime retail placement to labels and distributors that pay for it).

Again, this system led to the black and white "hit or miss" mentality of the past several decades. The good news is that the Internet and digital technologies have created an abundance economy where everything and everybody have equal access to the online marketplace. The only problem is, the online marketplace is flooded with products and noise of all kinds. It would be easy for consumers to become overwhelmed and confused by all the choices.

That's where "post-filters" come in. Music fans don't have to wade through everything to find the gems. They simply use some new tools and trusted sources to help them sort through it all.

Here are just some of the post-filters that fans use today to find new music:

• **Friends** – personal recommendations from familiar people will always be the leading way that consumers discover new music, books, films, and more.

• **Customer reviews** – being able to read what other people think of a given album on Amazon or CD Baby influences a lot of purchase decisions.

• **Popularity lists** – they come in all shapes and sizes: most downloaded, top sellers, highest rated, most discussed.

• **Blogs and podcasts** – the new niche tastemakers are bloggers and podcasters who cater to narrow audiences.

- **Genre-specific resources** – From AllHipHop.com to Rockabilly Radio, people gather where their main interests are addressed.

- **Search** – when in doubt, fans "Google" their favorite genres and see what comes up.

Your job as a music marketer is to tap into these sources. To make the best use of post-filters, do the following things:

- Encourage your current fans to share your music with their friends – and make it easy for them to do so.

- When a fan sends you a glowing email about your new album, ask them to post their comments as a review on Amazon, CD Baby and more – and give them the links where they can do that.

- Ask all of your fans to go to a certain site on the same day and vote you to the top of one of the popularity charts.

- Search for the terms your fans use to find music like yours and examine the sites that come up – then try to gain exposure on the top websites you discover.

5) Practice open-source promotion

Another offshoot of this evolution is the blurring of the lines between people who produce creative content and those who consume it. Case in point: The Beastie Boys once gave digital camcorders to 50 fans at a show in New York City and asked them to record everything they saw. Band member Adam Yauch combined his favorite bits from the 100-plus hours of footage into a feature film.

Members of the band O.A.R. tapped their fans to help them write an original song from scratch. Their Twitter songwriting contest encouraged fans to submit lyric ideas in 140 characters or less. The band chose six winners who contributed words for three verses, a chorus, a bridge, and the song title. The completed track, called "Light Switch Sky," was later released with proceeds going to a Paralyzed War Veterans charity.

Other examples:

- **Janet Jackson** held a "Design Me" cover contest for her album *20 Y.O.* and invited fans to submit potential artwork. She picked four of her favorite designs and used them in the U.S. pressing of the CD.

- **Barenaked Ladies** made the ProTools tracks to four of their songs available to fans and encouraged them to do their own remixes of them.

This open, collaborative approach is a stark contrast to the typical major-label stance of protecting copyrights at all costs and suing customers for illegally downloading music. These days, the smartest musicians, managers and indie labels are redefining what intellectual property and promotion are.

In this new era, artists don't always create in seclusion while fans passively sit and wait to be fed the latest music. Now everyone has an opportunity to express themselves. Use this to your advantage. Co-create with your fans. Ask them to help you produce videos, artwork, T-shirt designs, even alternate versions of your recorded music.

There's another benefit to this that's worth mentioning. One of the things you hear unsigned, independent artists complain about is the lack of a team or staff to help them market effectively. They think the only solution is to spend a lot of money on publicists and virtual assistants.

The truth is, once you start attracting even a small fan base, you can invite these supporters to create and promote with you. This direct involvement will create stronger bonds with your fans, which will spread to more fans and even more involvement. Done right, you can grow an army of fans who are eager to promote you. It will lead to a more organic and authentic growth rate ... and it won't cost a lot of money.

Bottom line: Get fans involved and allow them to be co-creators in your success story!

Now you have the five main principles of Internet music marketing. Focus on them and you will see more results, more fans, and more money.

Chapter 6

The Guerrilla Marketing Online Fan-Attraction Formula

Let's continue our exploration of Internet music promotion by introducing you to a new concept: "Octopus Marketing." It's a term I coined with my friend Scott Ginsberg some years ago. If you've ever caught one of my live workshops, there's a good chance you heard me discuss my Octopus Marketing Formula. But this is the first time I've included this simple but powerful concept in a book.

Here's the basic premise behind it ...

Think about the shape of an octopus. This unusual sea creature is comprised of a head that sits in the middle. Extending out from this body mass in the center are several tentacles that reach out in all directions.

I realize this is an oversimplification of what an octopus is (my apologies to any offended marine biologists out there), but it serves as a great visual analogy to describe the online marketing formula I recommend.

Using the octopus shape as a reference, the "head" of your online operations should be your own artist (or music company) website. This is a site that you own and control. And it sits at the center of all of your Internet activities.

Important: Don't use Facebook (or whatever high-profile site is buzzing when you read this) as the primary online destination for your music. The center of your promotion efforts should always be your own website – where you own the domain name, you pay for hosting, you control the mailing list, and more.

Free profiles on high-traffic sites like Facebook (and before that, MySpace; and before that, MP3.com) are great and should be used to their full advantage. But these sites don't owe you anything. If your profile suddenly disappears (which has happened to many artists) or someone mistakenly reports you for abuse, you may have no recourse. And good luck trying to reach someone who can help restore your page.

All the time you spent building traffic and a large "friend" or "like" list can be taken from you in an instant. Your music career is too valuable to leave to chance. So purchase your own domain name (such as www.YourBandName.com) and create your own website – and make it the focus of your activities online!

Reaching out from your home base

What about all of the other sites you want to be on that offer free or low-cost profiles? You guessed it: Those are your tentacles. They are the places online where you reach out and set up camp. Consider them outposts that allow you to have a presence in the many places where your potential fans are hanging out on the Internet.

Returning to our Octopus Marketing theme, keep in mind that all of these external outposts are connected to your personal website "head" in the middle via tentacles.

To hammer this concept home (and just in case you're a little squeamish about aquatic creatures), let's extend the analogy. Think of a bicycle tire. At the center is the axle (your artist or company website). Extending out from the axle are many spokes that reach out to the tire rim.

In this light, you can think of effective online marketing as a hub-and-spoke system. Your personal website in the middle connects to all of the outposts that sit along the rim. Each outpost points back to your personal website. In addition, the outposts often point to each other. Everything is interconnected in a highly active marketing eco-system.

The Octopus Marketing Formula in Action

Okay. If you're still with me, let's take a look at how this conceptual system of hubs, spokes, tentacles, and tire rims might operate in the real world.

Let's say you just posted a new video clip on your artist website. To let people know, you go out to Facebook and publish the following update:

NEW VIDEO: Be one of the first to see what happened backstage Saturday night before our show in Chicago. I had no idea Randy could do that without breaking his arm – [web page link here]

(**Note**: Even though you may have uploaded this video to YouTube, in this example you have "embedded" it on a page on your artist website, which is where the link above takes people.)

Sheila, a fan from Chicago who didn't make your show there, is on Facebook and sees your update. Intrigued, she clicks the link. It takes her to your website, where she watches the video and laughs out loud.

While on your site, Sheila notices that you are giving away three free song downloads to anyone who joins your online fan club. She was already a casual fan who followed you on Facebook, but seeing the video made her feel a stronger connection to the band. So she enters her name and email address and signs up.

On top of that, Sheila goes to your contact page and sends you a personal message saying how much she enjoyed the video and how she hopes to catch you live the next time you perform in town. The next day, you send her a quick email reply thanking her for the kind words and letting her know you hope to meet her on your next swing through Chicago.

A week later you send an email update to your entire fan list. In the email, you include a link to a page on your website where you just posted a short audio of a new song you are working on. You ask fans to give it a listen and leave some feedback.

Sheila checks her email and finds your latest message in her inbox. She opens it and, since you replied to her email and entertained her so much with that video the week prior, she clicks the link to listen to your new musical work-in-progress.

Of course, that link sends Sheila to your website again, where she listens to the new song and leaves a comment about it. While on your site, she notices you have a link to your Twitter account. She's been slowly warming up to Twitter and using it more lately to follow her favorite celebrities and stay connected with friends.

Sheila logs into Twitter and starts following you. While there she posts this update:

You gotta check out [band name] at [web address] – great songs, and they're hilarious too!

Brian, an old college friend of Sheila's, happens to catch her tweet about your band. He clicks the link, goes to your artist site, and starts listening to some of your streaming music samples. He loves the songs and also subscribes to your free fan club mailing list.

As luck would have it, Brian has a blog on which he publishes random thoughts, including posts about new music he has discovered. A few days later, he publishes a short piece about your band and how much he enjoys it. He then logs into LinkedIn, a site he uses often, and posts an update with a link to his latest blog post.

Michelle, a graphic designer who has done business with Brian, sees his LinkedIn update, clicks the link, and reads about your music on his blog ...

And so the cycle continues.

Enter the Marketing Communication Triangle

This fictitious story is a pretty accurate representation of the way things ideally and organically play out online. As you can see, it's a multilayered process that includes activity in many directions. It involves you posting interesting things on your website, along with you sharing links to those pages on various social networking sites.

Many of the things you post across the Web via your outposts will motivate people who follow you to click the links you include (or at least comment on the status update you posted).

In addition to the back-and-forth communication you have directly with your fans, you will ideally inspire your followers to share your links with their friends, thereby creating a communication triangle – artist to fan, fan to artist, and fan to fan.

Here are the five critical factors that make this system truly work for you:

1) Create a solid website hub

Since your personal artist or music company website is at the center of your online activities, it should be well designed. That doesn't mean it has to be flashy or expensive, but it should be easy to understand and navigate. If visitors become confused or find it difficult to maneuver around, they will quickly go elsewhere.

Another book in this series, *Guerrilla Music Marketing Online*, has an entire chapter dedicated to creating an effective artist website. So I won't repeat everything covered in that resource. Just know that your website should ideally be attractive and accurately represent the identity you want to get across.

It should also be designed in a way that gives fans what they need (perhaps song samples, a live show schedule, photos and videos, info on who you are) while leading visitors to the actions that are important to you (like getting on your fan email list, purchasing music, attending shows, liking your Facebook page).

2) Have a way to capture fan names and email addresses

I've been preaching this for years, but it's amazing how many artists overlook this powerful form of fan communication. So here is another loud pronouncement reminding you how important it is to build a mailing list. It's an essential part of this Octopus Marketing strategy – which is why I recommend you create a clear and compelling incentive to sign up for your free email updates. And put that incentive on every page of your website!

With a large and growing mailing list, you have a direct way to contact fans and stay on their mental radar screens. Research has proven time and time again that artists (as well as entrepreneurs and businesses of all kinds) get the biggest responses from relevant and enticing messages sent by email to their customers and fans.

Design your website in such a way that a clear and compelling offer to join your list is on every page. Ideally, that offer should be more than a simple "Get on our email list" plea. Take things a step further and create some allure surrounding what fans get when they submit their name and email.

In fact, the smartest musicians don't even refer to it as a mailing list. They call it a VIP Club or Backstage Pass. People don't just subscribe, they become "members" of this elite group of fans. Offer your members special perks like free downloads, discounts, advance access to new songs, invites to pre-show meet and greets, and more. And all they have to do is submit their name and email address to get all these goodies.

There are many options for managing your mailing list. I suggest you not do it manually yourself. Use a service such as **ReverbNation.com** or **FanBridge.com**. If you use **HostBaby.com** or **Bandzoogle.com** for your website hosting, both have built-in email list services. You might also consider **TinyLetter.com**, **MailChimp.com**, **ConstantContact.com**, or **Aweber.com**.

3) Set up your online outposts

Once your artist website hub and mailing list are in place, the next step is making sure you have solid tentacles leading to your online outposts (pardon the mix-and-match analogies here). At the end of this chapter I'll suggest some specific places at which you should have accounts, and most of them are free.

The main thing to keep in mind here is that you will at some point need to spend a little time fleshing out your profiles on these various social and music websites. If you're just starting out, go ahead and open an account at each site and try to grab a consistent customized web address at each, such as YouTube.com/yourbandname and Twitter.com/yourbandname.

If you already have established accounts at the outpost sites you want, it's a good idea to take a fresh look and see if your profile at each one should be updated. Perhaps your bio or "about" section is no longer up to date, or maybe you neglected to link to your artist website and other social sites across the Web. In addition, these sites add new features and roll out redesigns all the time, so it's a smart thing to check in every now and then to make sure you are making the best current use of each site.

4) Be proactive and consistent at posting updates across multiple sites

Okay. You have a solid hub and spoke system set up and you're ready to rock. Now you must get in the habit of regularly writing, posting and circulating updates. In the next chapter we'll cover a lot more specifics about what to post, but the main thing you must do now is make a commitment to posting something every day – multiple times a day would be even better.

To get more mileage out of these efforts, you should cross-post many of your updates so they appear on multiple sites at once. The good news is, there are several sites and services that can help you automate this process. At the time of this writing, two good ones to explore are **Artist Data** (www.artistdata.com) and

Hootsuite (www.hootsuite.com). You can even use Hootsuite to schedule a series of updates ahead of time.

Important: All of these great sites and the entire Octopus Marketing Formula will amount to nothing if you don't use them. Stale social media profiles with no activity will not attract fans and build your notoriety! So figure out now how you will incorporate a consistent posting schedule into your lifestyle.

5) Make engagement, interaction and relationship building more important than one-way announcements

Just in case this hasn't sunk in yet, let me make this abundantly clear: Marketing is not about shouting to get people's attention. (Remember the blue bowling ball story?) It's not just about announcing your upcoming shows and letting people know you have stuff for sale. These things can be part of an overall communication strategy, but if that's all you do, I guarantee you will chase away more people than you attract.

You haven't spent all of this time and energy setting up this hub-and-spoke system just so you can make one-sided proclamations about your musical activities. Remember the communication triangle we talked about earlier in this chapter? The conversation flows in multiple directions – from you to your fans, from your fans to you, and from fan to fan.

Your job is to facilitate that multi-directional flow of ideas and self-expression. That means you must resist the urge to make all of your status updates about you. *Stop thinking of yourself as a music information dispenser and start assuming the valuable roles of conversation starter and community builder.*

Commit these three things to memory: engagement, interaction, and relationship building! Make them part of your new music marketing mantra.

An overview of your online tentacles

As I mentioned earlier, I'm using this book to introduce you to the essential principles of marketing. As you know, when it comes to technology and the Internet, things change at a rapid pace. So I am purposely going easy on listing too many specific sites, services and apps – since that info could well be outdated by the time you read this.

I do go into much greater detail in the *Guerrilla Music Marketing Online* book (which I plan to update more often than this one). However, to help you establish your tentacles (or hub-and-spoke structure), I will give you a few suggestions of established sites that seem to be in it for the long haul.

Must-have social tentacles

If many millions of people are using a particular site and you keep hearing about it, it's probably a good idea for you to have a presence on it. As I write this, here are some of the fundamental sites you should be on, regardless of your genre or how you are building your music career.

Facebook.com – As long as this mammoth site continues to be the social media juggernaut, you should be on it. I suggest using your personal profile for family and close friends, and starting a separate fan page to build your music career.

YouTube.com – Video consumption on computers and smartphones is off the charts. You really should create and publish video content every month. YouTube is by far the biggest of the video hosting sites (and it doesn't hurt that it is run by Google), but you might also look into Vimeo.com and Ustream.com.

Twitter.com – It's the quickest and easiest of the high-profile sites to set up and start using. And at a maximum 140 characters per post, there is really no good reason not to have an account here.

LinkedIn.com – This is the primary business networking site, and a lot of musicians and music biz pros are on it. Be sure to join topic- and genre-appropriate groups and interact within them.

Google.com – This online powerhouse has so many cool, free features (like Gmail, Calendar, Analytics, Drive, etc). At the very least, start a free Google account and get on Google+. If you have original music to sell, check out Google Play too.

High-profile music tentacles

As for music-specific destinations online, there are thousands. Here are some of my top picks.

If you have music for sale (whether original songs or covers that you have acquired the mechanical rights to sell, as either digital downloads or a physical album), you really should check out **CDBaby.com** and **Bandcamp.com**. Also, make sure your music is available for sale on **Amazon.com** (by going through **CreateSpace.com** or Amazon's Advantage program).

Whether you have music for sale or not, you should look into **ReverbNation.com**, **TopspinMedia.com**, **Nimbit.com**, **SoundCloud.com** and **FanBridge.com**. You don't have to be on or use all of these sites, but you should certainly be aware of them and choose the ones that make the most sense for you.

Genre and topic-specific tentacles

Beyond these primary social and music sites, you should ideally be active on sites that are specific to your unique musical style and identity. Some of these will include blogs, podcasts and "genre destination" sites that you will uncover by doing research online.

For example, if you play an Americana or Alt-Country style, you might want to frequent the Twang Nation blog. If you perform Cajun Zydeco music, then the Zydeco Zone podcast would be an ideal target. Likewise, Mele.com would be perfect if you produce Hawaiian or island music of any kind.

With this category of websites, you often won't be able to set up a profile like you do on the others. What you do instead is reach out to the people who run these niche blogs, podcasts and genre sites and get to know them. Leave relevant, helpful comments and share new artists and resources they might be interested in (hint: not just your own music).

Yes, there's a bit of work that goes into setting up an effective Octopus Marketing (or hub-and-spoke) system online. But once it's in place, you'll have a solid structure that will allow you to communicate with fans, your fans to connect with you, and your biggest supporters to share their enthusiasm with each other.

Do yourself and your music career a favor and start setting up yours now!

Chapter 7

Everything You've Always Wanted to Know About What to Post and Share Online to Promote Your Music

In the last chapter, we covered how to lay the foundation for building an online presence. If you accepted my advice (and I hope you did), you're sold on the idea of creating an Octopus Marketing (or hub-and-spoke) system with your artist website at the center. All of the other social and music websites you choose to be on extend out from your personal site. Everything is connected in a strategic "web" of interconnectivity.

Great. Understanding this framework is the first crucial step. The next step is actually setting it up – meaning, you create an attractive and effective website, and you flesh out your profile pages on the various sites you have chosen (Facebook, YouTube, Twitter, CD Baby, Amazon, and more).

Accomplishing these first two steps alone will put you way ahead of most independent artists and music companies. So if you've reached this point, congratulations!

Most people complain about a lack of time or make a half-hearted commitment to getting this structure in place, but they never quite get there. But not you. You are a determined musician and guerrilla marketer! And you do whatever it takes to set up a system that will help you share your music with more and more people who need to hear it.

That's awesome. You deserve to feel proud. But don't stop there. Now you need to put this infrastructure to good use. You must infuse it with the energy and communication flow that will lead to more of your ideal fans discovering you and telling their friends.

Don't let it go to waste!

Imagine that you spend months building the perfect home recording studio. You sound-proof the walls, install the latest recording equipment and microphones, and run all the wiring. Finally, it's complete.

Then ... you just let it sit there and rarely use it all.

It would be pretty foolish of you to waste all that effort and potential. Right? Don't make this same mistake when it comes to using the structure you've set up to build your online presence.

Okay. You're convinced. And you're now ready to get busy putting this new hub-and-spoke system to work. The two most common questions that come up at this point are ...

What sites should I focus on? And ... What do I post?

Those are great questions. Inquiring musicians want to know: What sites will deliver the most bang for your buck? And what do you communicate to your fans, friends, followers, and subscribers? Not knowing the right answers keeps a lot of self-promoting musicians from doing anything at all. Can you relate?

By the end of this chapter, you'll have a solid handle on where to spend your time and what types of things you should post as social media updates and messages to your fans. You'll also know how to tailor all of the many options to your strengths and personality.

The Three E's of Communication

In my never-ending quest to uncover the underlying principles behind effective marketing tactics, allow me to introduce you to some basic ideas about communication. I've had a passion for the written word since childhood and have spent a good portion of my life sharing my ideas with people in many forms. From this perspective, I can tell you that there are primarily three reasons that we communicate with other humans.

1) To Educate – With this basic form of communication, you impart information. This includes giving people facts they need to know, instructions on how to do something, directions, or some similar exchange of knowledge.

As a self-promoting musician, you might educate people on where you are playing this weekend, who your musical influences are, when your next album will go on sale, what techniques you use to create your sound, and more.

2) To Entertain – Here your goal is to give people a temporary mental vacation. Give them a good reason to smile or simply tap their toes and groove out for a few minutes.

An obvious way to entertain your fans would be to share a new song or music video. But you can also give people that brief mental vacation by posting a funny quote, sharing a witty observation, or uploading a silly photo of something strange that caught your eye while you were on the road.

You don't have to stick with just the facts. Give people something that will amuse them for a couple of minutes and they will be more likely to remember you.

3) To Enlighten – I chose the word "enlighten" here to remain consistent with the E-word theme. But an equally appropriate phrase would be "to inspire." With this type of communication your aim is to get people to think differently or give them an emotional charge that makes them feel better.

You can accomplish this with something as simple as an inspiring quote or as involved as a 900-word blog post about how you overcame a personal challenge and rose above it. You can post links to songs and videos (created by you or someone else) that include empowering messages, and much more.

You should keep these three communication goals in mind whenever you post a status update or send a message to your fans. If you can solidly accomplish just one of these things (educate, entertain or enlighten), you're doing well. But often you can combine themes and inspire and entertain people while you educate them. Then you'll be firing on all cylinders.

The Three Sensory Modes of Communication

Now that we've explored the three basic types of things to communicate, let's dive into the vehicles you'll use to deliver your messages. Once again, I've broken down this topic into another list of three. I know, many of these may seem obvious. But if you take the time to stop and consider these subtle differences, you'll make better choices and reach more fans online.

Here are the three basic methods you have to communicate online:

1) Text – Yes, the good ole written word is probably the most common way to get ideas across online. This category might include short tweets you post on Twitter, status updates you add on Facebook, articles you post to a blog, email messages you send to fans, and more. If you can write even moderately well, this is the easiest and most common way to communicate online.

2) Audio – This mode of communication is obviously absorbed by the ears. The typical way for musicians to use audio, of course, is to encourage people to listen to their songs. Let's face it, hearing your music is the primary way that people determine whether or not they "like" you.

Potential fans may be intrigued by a photo or a written description, but all that really matters in the end is how they feel about you once they have heard your music. As a self-promoting musician, you must put a considerable effort into motivating people to sample your songs and listen to your music.

But communicating via audio extends well beyond sharing your songs. It can also include spoken-word messages to your fans. Imagine how you would feel if you received an email from one of your favorite artists that included an audio option.

In addition to the normal text information included in the email, you found a link that said "Click here to listen to a special audio message from Trey, the lead singer."

Wouldn't that be more engaging than simple text?

Another option would be to produce your own podcast (which is basically an online radio show that people can subscribe to using iTunes or another podcast "catcher" service). To make the best use of this route, you should have a specific show topic or theme and keep a regular schedule when new episodes are published. More time and technical skills are required with a podcast, but it is a good audio option to consider.

3) Visual – The third and final communication mode involves reaching people through their eyes. This basically takes two forms – video and still images – so I will address them separately.

In case you didn't know, video has become one of the most popular ways that people absorb information online. So if you aren't using video of some form on a regular basis, you are missing out on some great opportunities to reach new fans and create a stronger bond with existing fans.

There are many ways you can communicate as a musical artist using online video. The obvious choice for musicians is music videos of your songs. Even these can take many forms: from slick cinematic productions to simple one-camera recordings of a live performance; from a collage of still photos set to your music to a "lyric video" that features the text of your verses as if they were subtitles.

Consider this: But there are many video formats beyond the music video. Some of your choices include: simple talking head recordings of you speaking directly into a webcam, interviews with the band, interviews with raving fans, sneak peeks at life on the road or backstage, interviews you conduct with other artists, glimpses of your latest recording session, and more.

While video is king, don't overlook the visual impact of still images. These can include shots taken from your latest promotional photo shoots or live shows. They can also be still photo versions of some of the video ideas in the previous paragraph: Pictures of your fans, life on the road, backstage peeks, recording sessions, etc.

Additional ways to use visuals online: Upload images of your album artwork, gig posters, T-shirt designs, stage banners ... anything that will catch the attention of distracted fans online and motivate them to spend a few extra moments seeing what you're up to.

What's Your Communication Style?

There's a good reason I gave you the preceding two lists related to online communication. Because now you will use that basic knowledge to start determining the types of things you will post online, along with the best formats to use.

Here's the big question you need to answer: *What is your strongest communication mode or style?* Answering that will help you narrow down the way you communicate online.

Are you a good writer? Do you have a passion for (or at least a sincere interest in) the written word? If so, then text-based forms of communication may be a big part of your future. If you dread writing and consider it a burden, or if your grammar skills are horrendous, than you probably won't make a text-based blog a big part of your marketing game plan.

Are you a good conversationalist? Can you express yourself well verbally when speaking off the cuff? Do you sound natural when reading from a script or prepared notes? Have you ever dreamt of hosting your own radio show? If you answered yes to any of these questions, then audio messages or a podcast might be an effective way for you to deliver your message.

What about video? When you speak into a camera lens, do you look and sound natural? Or do you feel awkward? Have you ever dreamed about being a roving reporter? Or does the idea of being captured on video horrify you? How you answer these questions will help determine how you use video content and how often.

There's no cookie-cutter right answer here. Some people mumble through social conversations but are brilliant and engaging with the written word. Some people never honed their skills at prose but are powerfully effective when speaking into a microphone. Even if someone is articulate using the spoken word, that doesn't mean it will translate well to an on-camera presentation.

Your job right now is to determine where your strengths lie in these areas. Then make a commitment to using the communication mode that suits you the best.

A word of warning: Your current discomfort level with one mode or the other should not be confused with your potential ability. It's quite natural the first time you hear a recording of your speaking voice or see yourself on video to be surprised. "Oh my, do I really sound like that?" or "I hate seeing myself on camera."

If you have an inner feeling that either audio or video communication is right for you, start getting practice out of the public eye. I did a lot of on-camera work in college classes and personal projects with friends long before I hosted a local cable music video show many years ago. When I moved to the more public platform of the video show, I was far from perfect. But by then I had moved past the early awkward stages of speaking into a camera. And by doing it regularly, and carefully watching and learning from the playback of my recorded segments, I continued to get better.

So make the best use of your existing communication strengths, and take steps to hone the skills that you feel will serve you best moving forward. Knowing what your strongest skills are in these areas will help you answer this common question:

If I have limited time (and who doesn't these days?), what sites should I focus on?

If the written word is your strength, then perhaps **Wordpress.com**, **Blogger.com** or **Tumblr.com** would be best for you. If it's spoken-word audio, you might make **Soundcloud.com** or your own podcast the main focus of your efforts. If the video format is your thing, then **YouTube.com** or **Vimeo.com** would be obvious sites to invest time in.

Important note: Even if you choose one or two sites or mediums to dominate, you still should have a presence on many other social sites and use them to direct attention to your core format.

Another thing: Even if you host your media files on a specific site (such as YouTube for videos or Soundcloud for audio), you should still embed the players on your own website. That way, people can discover you on the hosting site itself, but when you post links for your fans and followers, you should ideally send them to your artist website to listen, watch or read what you have created.

Great. You're totally onboard with everything you've read to this point. But you may still be asking ...

Now that I have this system set up, what do I post?

Don't feel bad. It's a common question, often followed by a statement like "I don't have anything to say" or "No one cares what I'm doing." And it's this uncertainly that leads many artists to either do nothing (not an option for you) or to start making announcements like, "Hey, I'm playing this Friday at Mel's" or "New songs available on iTunes – buy now!"

You can do better. And you will do better once you read over the following list of content suggestions. Note that "content" here refers to anything you create: text, audio or video. Keep in mind that just about all of the examples that follow can be created in any of those three formats. So as you look over the list, think about how you can apply each idea to your communication style and strength.

Original content – This is obviously stuff you create yourself from scratch. It might be a blog post about an event that inspired your latest song or a short video asking people to come to your next gig in a certain city. It can be an album review of your favorite band's new CD, a commentary on something that's hot in the news, photos of your new guitar, or a look inside your band's touring van. If it was written, shot or recorded by you, it's original content.

Curated content – This is the thing that a lot of musicians overlook. You don't have to actually create everything you share with your friends and followers. Who has that kind of time? One thing that smart online marketers do for their fans is "curate" content – which is just a fancy way of saying that they find helpful stuff that their customer's might enjoy and link to it.

For example, I'm best known for being a source of music marketing ideas for self-promoting artists. Therefore, a lot of my social media updates are simply links to helpful articles, blog posts, videos and podcasts on music promotion. Some of them I wrote or recorded myself but many were created by other people.

By doing this, people in my target audience come to view me as a trusted source of information on my topic. I act as a filter that helps them find some of the best content out there on music marketing (whether I produced it or not). And, over many years of consistently doing this, my reputation is enhanced.

You can do something similar as a musician. Whatever your specific style of music is, you can start pointing people to the best articles, reviews, videos, interviews, and events related to your musical style and the artists who are making waves within it. Doing so, you'll attract more fans of the genre.

Of course, you'll also sprinkle your updates with links to your own musical activities. But by thinking beyond your own immediate needs and positioning yourself as a resource on your genre, your notoriety will grow a lot faster than it would otherwise.

Questions – One of the big buzzwords in recent years has been "engagement." What that means is, you ideally want people to interact with your messages and not just silently view them from the sidelines. One of the most direct ways to inspire engagement is to ask a question.

For you that might be "What's your favorite love song of all time?" or "What is your favorite smooth jazz album?" Or you might ask, "How long should a drum solo be?" or "What are the first three songs you can think of that have a color in the title?" You can also ask nonmusical questions such as "If you came back as a Crayon, what color would you be?" (I actually asked this question on Facebook once and got dozens of comments.)

Fill in the blank – Similar to questions, another powerful thing you can post is a sentence that you ask your fans to complete. Examples: "Early to bed and early to rise, make a _____" or "I love the smell of _____ in the morning." I find it helps to actually include "Fill in the Blank" at the beginning of these types of updates.

Personal updates – While many of your updates and messages to fans will be about your music, you should also consider sharing glimpses into your personal life. This shows you are human and will help fans feel they know you as a person as well as an artist. Only you can decide how much to reveal about your family, your home, and your personal beliefs, but an occasional peek at your offstage life could help you bond with fans.

Funny or heartfelt observations – If you have a sense of humor, share your wit online. Oftentimes the funny things you say to your friends or to yourself should stay private, but sometimes they may be worth sharing with fans. Whether it's a comment about someone you are stuck behind in a grocery store check-out line or your opinion of the quarterback's lousy performance in the big game, consider posting some of these humorous things online. The same thing applies to more serious and touching experiences you have. If you're laughing, smiling or crying about something, there's a good chance other people will too.

Quotes – When you're really coming up blank for something to post online, you can't go wrong with a funny or inspiring quote. Even though it seems at times that they are overdone, I can tell you from my own experience, quotes get shared and commented on a lot. There are countless websites dedicated to quotes, so you won't have any trouble finding good ones with a quick search.

Straight promotion and sales – I saved this for last, not because it's unimportant, but because I wanted to put it in its proper place. Some aggressive promoters think that everything you post online should be selling something. That's a short-sighted attitude. Other timid artists are afraid to market themselves or sell at all. That's a poor strategy too.

The key is finding a balance. I don't suggest you get too worried about percentages, but a basic rule of thumb might be: for every 10 things you post, make three of them promotional in nature – announcing an upcoming gig, letting fans know where they can buy your music, asking people to sign up for your free email list, etc.

When you have a big event taking place, the percentage of promotional messages will be higher, and that's fine. During periods of slower music activity, they might be lower. The main thing is to keep posting updates and sending emails to your fans and to continue creating content of some kind for your followers.

Keep the communication flowing

This is a point that deserves repeating: Even if you don't think you have much going on in a given week or month, continue to post regularly and stay visible throughout your hub-and-spoke system.

If you disappear for months until you have something big and bold to promote, you will have to reacquaint yourself with your audience. You will have to work that much harder to remind them of who you are and why they were attracted to you in the first place.

But if you consistently post cool new content of your own, point people to the best links related to your genre, and engage them with questions, fill-in-the-bank statements, quotes, and witty observations … they will be more involved with you and much more likely to jump in and support you when you have something really big to promote and sell.

That's the whole key to this Octopus Marketing Formula – you must use it to create awareness, make meaningful connections with fans, and leverage those relationships to spread your music to even more people.

Chapter 8

How Pomplamoose and Karmin Used YouTube and Social Media to Build a Huge Fan Base

So far in this section we've covered many important Internet and digital marketing strategies. Now let's dive into some concrete examples of artists who have used these principles to propel their careers.

In this chapter I will focus on two acts that just happen to be duos – Pomplamoose and Karmin. They each took different routes with their overall careers, but they both used online mediums (particularly YouTube) to initially create awareness and get the attention of fans and industry people alike.

Let's start with Pomplamoose ...

How a Beyonce hit helped launch an indie music powerhouse

Jack Conte and Nataly Dawn met in 2006 and soon formed a musical partnership. In 2008 they started a YouTube channel as Pomplamoose and began posting videos of their original songs. The duo got a modest boost when their song "Hail Mary" was featured on YouTube's home page. Then, in 2009, a simple shift in their approach led to a quick expansion of their audience.

In the summer of 2009 Jack and Nataly produced an album for Julia Nunes, an independent artist who had made a splash posting videos of herself doing cover songs on YouTube.

"We had this revelation," Nataly says. "We got the chance to observe her model and came to the realization that cover songs were really important when it came to getting your name out there. People don't know to search for your original songs, for the most part. But they will search for a song they want to hear on YouTube and, if you're lucky, they'll come across your stuff, like it, and go look at your original material."

"You have to do something to help people find you," Jack adds. "In the end, it's a matter of search engine optimization (SEO). If you have a multi-million dollar marketing machine behind you, then you don't have to work so much on SEO because the word is out there wherever people get their news."

He adds, "But if you don't have access to that machinery, you have to figure out how to get noticed in some other way. And for an indie musician, SEO, particularly on YouTube, is probably the most effective means of doing that. That means simply latching on to a cultural phenomenon, whether it's music or news related – anything that is current – and getting lots of searches. YouTube was our medium of choice."

That strategy worked. Within weeks of completing the Julia Nunes project, Pomplamoose posted their cover version of "Single Ladies" by Beyonce. Not only was it an unusual musical take on the song, but Jack's quick-cut video editing made it visually appealing as well.

The video started getting thousands of hits and soon went viral. "Our fan base quintupled within a couple weeks," Nataly says. "That cover song revelation was the most important part of our success so far." The video now has many millions of views.

Attention leads to sales and more attention

The exposure that the "Single Ladies" video generated led Pomplamoose to record and post more cover songs in their unique style. Sales of both their cover renditions and original songs began growing on iTunes. The following year both Toyota and Hundai featured Pomplamoose songs in TV commercials, and their notoriety grew even more. They were soon selling more than 100,000 downloads a year.

Most of the major labels have contacted them with offers to sign a deal, but thus far they are determined to remain independent. They seem quite happy with the level of "demi-celebrity" success they have achieved on their own.

"We're not famous," Jack says. "But you have to admit that at some level we are public-ish figures. A lot of people have heard of us, we get recognized on the street, people ask to have a picture. We have some level of that."

Pomplamoose has also broken a number of the so-called "rules" of music success. For the first three years of their existence on YouTube – as the duo was racking up millions of views, more than a 100,000 downloads, and national TV commercials – they never sold a physical product and rarely performed live. The prevailing wisdom is that an act has to tour and sell CDs and merchandise to survive. Not so for Jack and Nataly.

But they admit that not many years ago the tools to reach a mass audience were not available to most independent artists.

"It used to be that all the fortune and fame was in the hands of a few," Jack explains. "There were 20 great acts that everybody knew and listened to. They had all the recognition, sales and everything. Now that has been diffused into the hands of the many. Now we have thousands of demi-celebrity bands that are not super famous, but they're making a living, are happy, and are making the art they like. No one is sticking toes in their creative pies. They don't have to worry about being dropped by a record label. And I think it's a great transition."

You can do this yourself

Many musicians still think of achieving success on their own terms as something that is out of reach. As Nataly explained during an interview with NPR, "People think that all these things have to be done by geniuses behind huge desks at the top of a skyscraper. But you can just go online and do it yourself."

When I ask her to expand on that idea, she says, "If you have drive and you're creative, and if you want to make a living as an artist, it is totally possible. The music industry wants you to believe that a lot of things are exclusive, that they still hold the keys. But those things are very limited at this point. Like licensing, for example."

Both Jack and Nataly explain how easy it is to use an online service such as **Limelight** (www.SongClearance.com) or the **Harry Fox Agency** (www.SongFile.com). You search for the song you want to cover, fill out some online forms, and pay a modest fee to sell your recorded version of it.

"For people who aren't interested in being a star and just want to make a good living making the music they want to make, you absolutely don't have to go through a label," Jack adds.

How a wedding band singer from Nebraska and a trombone player from Maine became pop superstars

Amy Heidemann and Nick Noonan met in 2004 when they attended Berklee College of Music in Boston. She was a pastor's grandkid from Nebraska who grew up loving rap and hip-hop music. He was a musician from northern Maine whose main instrument was the trombone. Amy sang in a Boston wedding band to get through college, but by 2005 she and Nick were dating and collaborating musically.

"We did a few club gigs as a duo, but playing live in venues wasn't our scene," Nick says. "So we started performing on the street a lot." That's where they started honing their musical chops – with Amy on guitar and Nick playing a box-shaped percussion instrument called a cajon.

In 2010 the duo turned to YouTube and, like Pomplamoose, started posting videos of their originals songs using the name Karmin. Each of them had a pleasing look, a playful personality, and solid musical chops. But attracting fans was still a challenge. Then Nils Gums, an old friend who was getting into artist management, suggested something that would prove to be pivotal.

"He said we should record and post cover songs on YouTube, and do as many as we can," Nick explains. "So we started pumping out two videos a week and getting very active online. Nils also suggested we put as much personality as we could into the clips – you know, give them the Karmin treatment."

So they posted videos of cover songs by Lady Gaga, Adele, and many others. The viewer counts started going up, but the process was time consuming. "We spent countless hours editing those early videos," Amy says.

Experimentation leads to success

Then they tried something different: a single static shot of them playing the songs live. What you hear on the videos is what they played and sang on that take. No editing. "Those live videos got much more organic attention, for some reason," Amy says. "So we had to learn the hard way that the live stuff was much more popular. And way easier to record and post."

Then in April 2011 they posted a video of Chris Brown's "Look at Me Now" that took things to a whole new level. "It took off practically overnight," Amy explains. "There was an immediate buzz about it." The video started trending on the popular social news site Reddit. Musicians and industry people shared it. Ryan Seacrest soon featured it on his blog.

"We were getting 400 emails a day from fans and industry people," Nick says. "We had multiple laptops going to keep up, it was crazy." Within a few weeks, the duo was asked to perform "Look at Me Now" on *The Ellen DeGeneres Show*, which made the video go even more viral, leading to tens of millions of views.

When offers from major record labels came pouring in, they turned to their friend Nils to be their manager. In the summer of 2011, after a personal meeting with music biz impresario L.A. Reid, Karmin signed with Epic Records. In 2012 they released an EP, performed on *Saturday Night Live* and *Good Morning America*, and had a Top 40 hit single with "Brokenhearted."

The seeds of success

Obviously, their decision to use YouTube has been very good for Karmin. But they are quick to tell you that a lot of seeds had to be planted before their career sprung to life in such a big way.

"We posted 35 videos before 'Look at Me Now.' There was a lot of work that went into it," Amy says. "It was great having a catalog of stuff to show once we did get some major attention. When those millions of people saw 'Look at Me Now,' they had the option to go back and watch hours of content we had previously created."

"Remember, there was no label, no A&R helping us back then," Nick says. "We just figured out how to do it ourselves. That was the bottom line."

Amy poured herself into learning about marketing and social media. "I dove in," she says. "I didn't know how to use Twitter or Facebook. I learned everything from the ground up. We never paid for any marketing. I learned web design myself. We used to email every single YouTube subscriber and thank them."

Yes, it takes time, effort and dedication to make a dent with music fans. You have to be as creative with the marketing aspects of your career as you are with the music itself.

Amy adds, "An artist today has to be hungry and willing to do that, or you kinda don't have a shot. If you're not working every day communicating with people, being real, having conversations, and creating an online presence for yourself, someone else will outwork you."

Hopefully you now have a firm grasp and clearer picture of how to use the Internet to reach fans and get your songs into their ears, minds and souls. It can be a big and confusing undertaking at times, but it's well within your abilities to embrace it and use it well.

Next up: Music publicity and the many ways you can gain widespread media exposure. See you in the next section.

Section 3:
Guerrilla Music Publicity

Chapter 9

32 Ways to Get Exposure for Yourself, Your Band, or Your New Music Release

Despite what you may have heard to the contrary, promoting and marketing your music shouldn't be the dreary task so many people make it out to be. The pessimists tell us we have to shut down the creative side of our brains and shift into "business" mode. How dull. How boring. No wonder so many artists go running for the hills at the mere mention of having to promote their music.

What follows is a list of creative, low-cost ideas and techniques you can start using right away to get media exposure for your music. Read these tips. Think about them. Play with them. Have some fun with them. But, most important, put them into action ... starting today!

Translate your story into a newsworthy hook

Announcing the release of another new album won't get you very far. Music magazines get dozens of these ho-hum announcements every day. However, the debut release from a volunteer firefighter or a guy who can juggle three chainsaws at one time might catch the attention of a music editor. Why? Because it has a news "hook" that makes it stand out.

So what's your news hook? To uncover it, ask yourself these questions:

- Does your band name or new album title have a significant meaning?

- Have any of your members won awards, done brave deeds, or accomplished anything noteworthy (they don't have to be music-related)?

- Do the lyrics to any of your songs tie in with a current event or trend?

Lesson: Always be on the lookout for fresh news hooks related to your music and then share them with the media outlets most likely to cover them.

Here's a sampling of free press that artists have received in various publications over the years – along with the news hooks they used to get it:

1) The band Too Much Joy received a letter from former Speaker of the House Newt Gingrich letting the members know that the group's tune "Theme Song" had inspired countless Republican activists to pursue their conservative agenda during a recent election.

The only thing is, members of Too Much Joy never supported Gingrich and didn't consider themselves to be politically right leaning in any way. The *Aquarian Weekly* plastered its cover with the news item and filled up two full pages inside dealing with the issue.

Have you received a letter from a public figure? Could you write to someone well-known and request that they write a brief note about your music?

Another option: When a famous author comes to your town for a book signing ... buy the book, get in line, and ask him or her to write a special inscription – such as "The Lipsmackers Rock! -Dr. Phil." Take a photo of the signature and leverage it to get as many plugs in the media as you can.

2) The Texas-based band Rare Seed got a blurb in a local paper regarding its upcoming appearance on a regional music video program. This brings up an important point. Most musicians celebrate when they get covered in the media. And then they stop. These band members, on the other hand, used their success with television to lure the print media into also giving them a plug.

Why not use this cross-media technique with radio and Internet publicity sources too? Use every achievement as a stepping stone to your next marketing move. If done right, it's a never-ending process.

3) Dr. Frank, who fronts the Bay area band Mr. T Experience, received some press in *Bam* magazine regarding the "Dr." part of his stage name. It seems Frank was all set to attend graduate school at Harvard when he changed course to form a punk band instead.

Do you have an alternate career path you've either put on hold or are doing as a day job? If so, how can you squeeze some media exposure out of it? If the usual music papers and columnists don't nibble, what about trade publications or company newsletters associated with your other line of work?

4) The members of 1,000 Mona Lisas garnered a write-up concerning an incident that had them pulled over in Texas with state troopers searching them and their van for drugs. The band then called its next tour "Got Any Weed?" Now it's your turn ... not to get pulled over, but to take a frustrating situation and turn it into a promotional device.

What unusual things have happened to you lately? And how can you turn these experiences into a newsworthy advantage for your music?

5) What about the Accordion Babes Album & Pin-Up Calendar? That's what Renee de la Prade (known as "the squeezebox goddess") produces every year, with the help of several other female accordion players. It gets attention for a group of artists while also reinforcing her personal musical identity. Could you use this angle for your act?

6) The band Her Majesty the Baby got a blurb written because it was the first band on its indie label to release an album on a new, enhanced CD format. Do you have a unique way of presenting yourself that could be turned into a news item?

7) One hard-core Beatles fan got exposure when he persuaded the mayor of his city to declare December 8 as "John Lennon/Free as a Bird Day." Could you swing a similar proclamation?

8) A band I used to be in got coverage every year when we held our annual fundraiser for Our Little Haven, a children's charity in St. Louis. The media is often more receptive to covering events that benefit the community. And if you create a show that happens around the same time every year, you also create the opportunity for annual coverage, in addition to raising money for a great cause.

9) Silverwolf Records got coverage for its *Homeless Project*, a compilation CD of songs about the homeless. Does your album have a noteworthy theme? If not, could you give it one?

10) A rap trio whose members pack a few extra pounds performed a promotional workout at a New York fitness club. The media gathered and got photos and video of the rappers sweating to the sounds of their new single.

Now come up with your own news hooks. And remember, have fun doing it!

Blurbs, short takes and editorial mentions

Some people call them "blurbs." Others call them "short takes" or "brief editorial mentions." Whatever name you give them, they can add up to extra media exposure for you and your music. Feature stories and album reviews are great – and you should pursue these avenues of media coverage regularly. But what most music marketers overlook are the great opportunities that exist with music gossip columns, scene reports, industry updates, studio news, and more.

Reality: Every week, thousands of magazines, newspapers, websites, blogs and fanzines around the world need to fill certain sections with short, music-related items of interest. Since they're not especially prominent, these sections are often ignored by self-promoting artists and publicists. Don't overlook them.

What follows is a list of column blurbs I found while flipping through only a few regional music papers. Use these ideas to come up with your own list of angles to get regular "short take" news mentions.

11) The nostalgic R&B group the Fabulous Boogie Kings received some positive press after a club appearance in Houston. The blurb made a reference to the outstanding sales of the band's latest album. Do you have something of note to celebrate – an achievement that lends credence to your band's worth? If so, share it with the media.

12) Personality Crisis received a news blurb because the band was planning a special show to celebrate its 500th gig. Any special occasion – no matter how trivial it may seem to you – can be leveraged into a reason for a columnist or blogger to give you a plug.

13) A few Texas bands put together a traveling rock show package called the Divas of Rock Tour. Combining your efforts with other bands, record labels or a group of sponsors – and adding a theme – opens the door to more exposure.

14) Shaun Barusch got a few great media plugs when he formed MIA Records. Artists aren't the only subjects to get mentioned in the press. Consider your record label, distribution company, music charity, sound reinforcement company, recording studio – whatever – as a prime candidate for coverage.

15) Arts organization the Houston Music Council got press when it released a new volume of a compilation CD featuring local bands.

Now start thinking. Start writing down your ideas. Start getting exposure!

More creative music marketing ideas

16) Canadian entertainment lawyer Ryan Richardson worked with a band called Leaderdogs for the Blind, which released an album called *Lemonade*. Richardson says that when the record company did little to promote it, the band members decided to push their own singles – one being the title track, "Lemonade."

"Inserted with a flier promoting the singles was a small packet of brand-name lemonade drink mix that cost us a whopping five cents each," he says.

"Because the packages were so compact, there was no additional cost to mail them. Across the country, radio program directors and DJs apparently fought over who was going to keep the tasty beverage, and the singles ended up charting."

For most bands, this creative marketing ploy would have been enough. But not for the Leaderdogs.

Richardson explains, "At one of our summer festival shows, we distributed free homemade lemonade to the audience in 95-degree weather, as well as chilled cartons of the refreshment that had been donated by a local juice bottler for all of the industry types present. It worked well to reinforce the name of the song."

17) The Southern California band Saint Monday set up an in-store appearance at a Virgin Megastore location and gave away hundreds of free CD music samplers in five hours. Each sampler had a coupon for a $2 mail-in rebate that customers could get if they came back and bought the band's full-length CD at the store.

Since Saint Monday is promoting pop music with a fun and sexy image, the members are considering another creative tactic: giving away condoms with an inscription that reads "Saint Monday: Music That Turns You On."

So, what are you doing that's fresh and different to promote yourself as an artist? Not sure what creative marketing strategy to try next? Do this:

18) Sit down right now with a pen and notebook. Start brainstorming on every possible angle for a creative hook. Consider some of the aspects discussed in this chapter so far: the name of your band, the title of your new album, maybe even the subject matter of individual songs. Also think about current events and good causes you feel strongly about.

Ask yourself: "How can I take these details about my music and transform them into a newsworthy and attention-getting story?" Write down your answers. You might be surprised by the great ideas you uncover.

Create your own music events with others

You know the philosophy by now: *Don't wait around for music marketing opportunities to come to you. Instead, create the circumstances you desire by taking matters into your own hands*.

Nowhere is this more powerful than with music events you conceive and organize with other people. To illustrate the point, here are some possible avenues to pursue:

19) Throw a listening party. Gather together a group of bands and artists who have put out new albums recently. Find a nightclub or record store that's supportive of local music. Then ask for a date to hold a new music listening party.

On the night of the party, pick someone to emcee (maybe you) and introduce one act at a time, then play one or two tracks off of each band's album. At the end of each group's segment, you could have people in the audience ask the players questions.

You could also offer free (or cheap) food and drinks and discounted prices to anyone who wanted to buy any of the albums that night. It would be best to promote this as a safe, quick musical buffet for consumers who want to sample local music without having to hop from one beer-soaked club to another.

I wish more artists used this concept.

20) Present a collaborative, multi-act unplugged show. Sure, you could present an acoustic performance or songwriters circle with other musicians at a nightclub or record store. The format works ... but a lot of artists have done the same thing. It would be more interesting to take an extra step and stage an acoustic show like this at an unexpected venue.

Possibilities: art galleries, skate shops, hip clothing stores, recreation centers, shopping malls, bookstores, grocery stores, car dealerships, etc.

Once again, get a number of other acoustic acts on the bill and make sure the manager of the location is committed to actively promoting the event. Come up with a newsworthy theme and – combined with the offbeat location – you might have a nice angle with which to lure the media into covering it.

21) Tie into an already existing event. You don't have to create something completely new to make the most of events. You can also contact the organizers of already established events and ask if you could help them add a musical element. That way, they look good and you get exposure. Think about the many annual events in your region. Which ones would benefit from your talents and creativity?

Hot tip: If you can't formally get connected to an existing event, consider presenting an "unofficial" party at a nearby location. Many artists and labels do this during major music conferences such as South by Southwest. But you can do this to tie into any big event in any location.

Sneak into media exposure through the side door

22) Musician Laurie Z was once interviewed on a syndicated radio show called *Tech Talk*. The program features people who use modern technology in various fields. Past guests have included Tom Clancy, Kurt Russell and Todd Rungren. Laurie was invited to discuss how she's used technology to create her music and market herself.

The main thing to note in this example is that a musical act is getting media exposure on a non-music show – a valuable lesson for us all. How many potential avenues of promotion are you overlooking because you don't see an immediate connection between what various media cover and what you produce?

Here are some possible angles to get exposure on talk shows for different genres:

23) A jazz musician could team up with a psychologist or music therapist to discuss the stress-reduction benefits of mellow jazz music.

24) A traditional blues player who has either lived through or learned a lot about regional music history could pitch himself as an expert on local culture.

25) A punk or metal band member could become an advocate for safe mosh-pit etiquette and offer to enlighten kids and their parents on common-sense advice when attending concerts.

26) A rap artist might shed light on the fact that not all rap and hip-hop music is about gangs, sex and life on the streets.

27) A country musician could partner with a fitness instructor and espouse the virtues of line dancing as a fun form of exercise.

28) Become a music trivia expert. Do you know way too much about the Beatles? Or Elvis? Or the '70s, '80s or '90s? Or some other musical niche? If so, appoint yourself to be your area's media consultant on the topic.

Bottom line: You no doubt have many media exposure angles you have yet to use to your advantage. Now is the time to uncover them and put them to good use!

Still more music marketing tips to consider:

29) Keep in touch with your contacts. Make sure that at least once a month your fans and industry contacts get a phone call, post card, email, text, or other new message from you. Are you staying in touch with these people now? Your goal should be to regularly put your name and musical identity in front of the people who are in a position to support you.

Tip: Come up with a schedule that would accomplish more frequent contact with the people who matter most to your career. Add this to your monthly calendar.

30) Keep your ears open for ideas. Listen to the music-related things people complain about, and then provide a solution to their problem.

For instance, members of the Chicago band Cool Beans heard music fans complaining about all of the negative, angst-ridden lyrics in modern rock songs. Since they play upbeat alternative pop, they started using the phrase "Energetic new rock & roll ... without the angst!" on all of their marketing materials. Doing so positions them as the "alternative" to gloom rock. And they might not have used that approach if they hadn't listened to their fans.

31) Spell out your music for potential new customers. New Age artist John Huling puts a brief description of his music on the back of his CDs. By doing so, even customers who haven't heard his music before can get a quick synopsis of his style and what musical benefits he offers.

Lesson: Don't expect people to automatically know what your music is about. There is nothing wrong with indie artists putting review quotes and testimonials from happy fans on the back of CD sleeves and on their websites. Just be picky about which ones you use, focusing more on the quotes that spell out the heart of your musical message and the hard-hitting benefits listeners get when they hear it.

32) Make a commitment to do something every day to promote your music. If a day goes by that you don't do at least some small act to promote your music, you're cheating yourself. And the promotional action you take doesn't have to be earth-shattering. Simple actions are effective too – as long as they're done regularly.

Conclusion: Ultimate success in music comes as a result of the small steps you take consistently on a daily basis. Pick something covered in this chapter every day and put it to use. Doing so will earn you more fans, more notoriety, and more clout ... for weeks, months and years to come!

Chapter 10

Killer Press Kits: The 29 Key Elements of Sizzling Music Publicity Materials

Sometimes it's called a press kit. Other times it's referred to as a promo package or media kit. It can exist in the physical world or sit virtually on a website as an EPK (electronic press kit). Whatever you call it and whatever form it takes, this collection of music marketing tools will help you get more gigs, media exposure, radio airplay, industry attention, and more.

However, I should also remind you that over 95 percent of the press kits sent out by artists and record labels end up in the trash can (both the real world and online versions).

Reality: Those aren't very good odds. It's not easy to get pumped up when you consider that rate of failure.

But there's a good reason all those press kits are being ignored: Most of the promo packages clogging up the postal and email systems are lackluster attempts at marketing. They are hastily thrown together without much thought or purpose behind them.

I know this with certainty because for 10 years I published a music magazine in the Midwest. I've seen enough bad media kits to make anyone's head spin.

But I also recall the rare gems that caught my attention – the well-thought-out press kits that sold me on an act's worthiness, inspired me to give a song a quick listen, and quickly motivated me to assign a story on the act.

Action step: To make sure a lot more of your press kits are actually read and acted upon, please consider the following tips. These are what I consider to be the 29 most important elements of a successful promo package.

Soak up this advice and put it to use right away!

Cover Letter

Any time you submit a press kit, it should be accompanied with a cover letter or introductory email written to a human being at a publication, blog, radio station, booking agency, etc. This first element of your kit serves the all-important purpose of intriguing the recipient and spelling out the reasons he or she should bother looking through the rest of the kit.

Here are the main points to keep in mind when crafting this introductory letter:

1) Address the letter to a specific person

"Dear editor" won't cut it. Call, email or visit the publication's website and find out the exact name of the person who handles the area in which you want to make an impact. And get the correct spelling of that person's name!

2) It should be the first thing the person sees

When mailing a physical kit, place the cover letter on top. If the rest of the items in your press kit are neatly presented in a folder (which is a good idea), the cover letter should be paper-clipped to the outside of the front cover.

3) The cover letter should be no longer than one page

Make your letter relatively short and sweet. Lengthy, rambling messages and emails get set aside (or thrown away). Make your pitch quickly ... and then get out of the way. After all, it's the other elements of your kit that you really want the person to spend time reading and listening to.

4) It should speak directly to the person receiving it

Don't use your cover letter to brag about yourself. Instead, use it to show the recipient that you understand his or her position and the problems he or she faces. Then briefly describe why your musical story provides a solution and helps meet his or her needs.

Of course, if you've already communicated with the person before, point that out in the letter. If he or she has requested your material, make that very clear. If it's a cold submission, state your best case quickly and interestingly.

5) Write in a conversational tone

If I read one more "Per our telephone conversation ...," I'm going to strangle someone. Commit this tip to memory: Write like you talk. If you wouldn't say it that way to someone face to face, don't phrase it that way in a written message.

Let me clarify: Write like you talk, as long as you don't talk like an idiot. You must write your cover letter intelligently. Just don't try to sound overly professional to the point that you come across as pompous. People in the music business want to connect with other humans, not survey a document that reads like a college term paper.

6) Start with a sensible grabber

It helps when the opening sentence of your cover letter or email grabs the reader's attention.

Examples:

"Hi, my name is Fred and I manage a band called..." – BAD

"I'm sure most of the 800 people at our recent CD release party are readers of your fine paper." – BETTER (but it reeks of butt-kissing)

"When was the last time you heard a banjo player in a heavy metal band?" – BEST (this opening sentence is truly newsworthy, as long as there really is a banjo player in your heavy metal band)

Tip: You will never go wrong by starting out your first communication with a blogger or journalist with a specific compliment. Such as: "John, I want to let you know how much I enjoy your column. The piece you did last week on tattoos was hilarious! Your witty observations were spot on. The reason I'm writing is ..."

Note that the subject line of an email should also deliver a "grabber." Including the person's name and an indication of the email's purpose works well. Example: "Nick – idea for your Audio File column."

7) End with a P.S.

You should always have one or two major points, at most, to make in your cover letter. Take the most important point and repeat it in a P.S. along with a tempting call to action.

Example: "P.S. I know your readers appreciate being exposed to new trends in music. Heavy metal banjo players aren't exactly a dime a dozen. Please email or call me at the number below for more details. I'll even send you a free Banjomania T-shirt!"

News Release

A news release (also known as a press release) is a page that spells out the nitty-gritty on a specific event or newsworthy topic. Typical subjects include a new album release, a special upcoming show, or a personal appearance at a record store. News releases can also alert the media about upcoming TV show appearances, when a band reaches a noteworthy radio or sales chart status, info on a departing or new band member, etc.

Here are some tips to keep in mind when writing a news release:

8) Make it no longer than one page

Again, brevity is king. Lay out the important facts swiftly and simply. Don't make your readers wade through paragraph after paragraph of useless verbiage.

9) Limit the scope to one angle

A news release shouldn't tell your life story. It should cover only one sliver of your activities. Don't write a release about your new album *and* the band's new singer *and* the charity show next month. Craft a separate news release for each topic.

10) Put the meaty details up front

The traditional advice on news releases says to include the who, what, where, when, and why in the first paragraph. If you can do that in an interesting way, go for it. I'm not such a stickler for that wisdom, but do get to the point early and make sure all basic questions about your topic are answered somewhere in the news release.

Important note: There are many times when creating an official news release is not needed. If your story idea can be conveyed in a simple, conversational email to someone, there's really no need to write a formatted press release.

Another effective strategy is to send a quick note that grab's the attention of a journalist, then provide a link to the official news release posted online.

Artist Bio

As you should know, "bio" is short for "biography." An effective artist bio gives more detailed background information on the act and spells out the current state of things with your music. Here are the five elements of a good artist bio:

11) A bio should be no longer than two pages

While an artist bio can take up more room to tell your story, don't think of it as an encyclopedia. I've seen many bios that run a few pages, but these usually contain more facts than a media person needs to know. One or two pages at the most is plenty of space to share your musical life.

12) The best band bios read like magazine articles

Like many of the editors you'll be contacting, I enjoy reading bios that have the feel of a feature story in a newspaper or magazine. I don't want a long list of facts and accomplishments. I also don't care for a chronological résumé listing of your life story. But I do like to discover those things as I read an interesting tale about your music.

The best bios start off with a vivid description of the music, the artist's personality, and what the act is currently doing. Once those details are established, then you can give a little history and background on the main players.

13) Use quotes from key people

A good feature story-type of bio will intersperse exposition with quotes from the main player (or players) in your act. If there is another party involved in your story (such as a nightclub, charity or studio), get quotes from a person at that establishment too. Weaving in positive quotes from published reviews is also acceptable within a bio.

14) Be positive, but don't over-hype

Your bio should definitely put a positive spin on your musical activities. However, crossing the line and being too boastful can work against you. Writing that your band "has been causing a stir in Chicago with energetic live shows" is cool. Saying you're "the hottest thing since the Beatles and Elvis combined" is downright silly.

15) Write your bio as if a publication might run the entire thing

There's another reason to go easy on the hype. Many small publications may run some or all of your bio as an article. Most people who run music magazines, websites and blogs are overworked and underpaid. And there is always a shortage of well-written material to run. Give them something that's cleanly worded and interesting, and they just might run it as is.

Recorded Music

Your goal with media people is similar to your goal with fans. You want to motivate them to take the time to listen to your music. Listening to – and then enjoying – your songs is what turns casual listeners into diehard fans and indifferent editors into media cheerleaders for your music. Follow the suggestions in this section to improve your chances of getting your music heard by the media.

16) Take off (or at least slice open) the shrink-wrap

It may seem like a minor thing, but it does take some effort to pry off that impenetrable plastic that surrounds new CDs. Imagine being pressed for time and having to wrestle with a dozen (or more) of these babies at one sitting. Make it easy for people to enjoy your music and you will be rewarded!

Note: If you want to reach a lot of media sources and simply can't afford to send everyone a CD, do this: Send CDs to your high-priority contacts, people who have requested them, and sources most likely to cover you. Send your low-priority contacts an email with a link to your EPK and song samples. Let these people know you would be happy to send a physical CD if they ask for one. That way, you'll send CDs only to media people who really want them.

17) Make sure contact info is on the CD itself *and* the case it came in

I'll admit it, I'm a contact information freak. If you're going to be a lean, mean, self-promotion machine, you must do everything you can to get people (both industry folks and fans) to connect with you. Sending out your press kit and then expecting people to jump through hoops to figure out how to get in touch with you is pure madness.

Reality: Cover letters get separated from bios. Photos get removed from related news releases. CD sleeves drift away from the discs they identify. Put your contact info on everything! Think of your music marketing tools as frisky puppies that love to break from the leash and run away. They need identification tags so the people who find them know who they belong to.

18) Include a specific call to action

Put yourself in the shoes of the average blogger, editor or music writer. You are probably behind on a deadline, have a thousand things clamoring for your attention, and have a few dozen more acts emailing and sending you music in the mail.

Now imagine a typical musician who writes something like "Hey, my new album is out, and I think you'll really like it. Enclosed is a CD for you to check out (or here's a link where you can listen to the whole 12-song album online). Enjoy!"

Great. This artist is being proactive, which is more than most musicians do. But compare the previous message to this one:

"Hi John, I love your blog and the way you smartly dissect all the folk music albums you review. I'm a big fan. In fact, I just released a new album of my own that I think you'll really enjoy. If you're pressed for time – and who isn't these days – check out tracks 3 and 5 on the enclosed CD (or here are links to the two tracks I know you'll enjoy the most)."

See the difference? Again, make it easy for media people. Respect their time. Direct them to the songs you feel they would resonate with the most. And make a specific request for them to do so!

19) Don't forget the power of video

As you know, your goal is to get journalists to listen to your songs, while they learn more about you. These are important steps that will help them decide whether or not to write about you. One of the most captivating ways to consume sounds and information is via video. So be sure to point media people to your more alluring and popular videos. Provide a direct link and ask them to take a quick look to get a feel for who you are and what you sound like.

Photos

Another one of your goals is to help media people put a face to your name and sound. A good artist photo will do that. But good photos are rare. When you do have an intriguing, professional-looking photo, media people remember you – and your photo ends up in print and online more often. Here are some artist photo tips to consider:

20) Close-ups are better than wide shots

The best photos, generally speaking, are up close and personal. A tight shot on the members' faces is far more appealing than a wide-angle view of a band running through a field. And if you're a solo artist, you should definitely use photos with a close-up view. Keep the shapes and images in your photos simple and large – let them fill up the frame.

21) Keep backgrounds simple

The emphasis in your photo should be on the artist. But you'd be shocked by the number of pictures I've seen that feature musicians posing in front of busy, mind-numbing background scenes. After all, it is called an *artist* photo, not a background photo. Picking a location that has atmosphere and texture is cool, as long as you make sure that you and your band members stand out against it.

22) Avoid straight lines and dull arrangements

If your photographer asks you and your band mates to stand in an orderly, straight line while he or she shoots at eye level, run the other way. Don't do this, unless you plan on giving out smelling salts with all of your photos.

Better approaches: Stagger the positions of the players. Try sitting or laying down. Have the photographer shoot from a high angle above or low angle below. Or play with special effects lenses (as long as the visual effects don't blur the people in the picture too much).

23) Dress and pose members so they look like they're in the same band

Did you ever see the "We Are the World" charity video from the 1980s? You had rockers and R&B players standing next to pop stars and folk singers. That's great for a cooperative charity event, but it's plain lousy for your band photo. Unfortunately, way too many band photos have this disjointed, mix-and-match feel.

Long before the photo shoot, every member should have a handle on what identity the band needs to portray. Dress accordingly. Attitudes and facial expressions also need to gel. One guy can't be scowling while another sports a goofy grin. Bottom line: Have a consistent look and vibe.

24) Supply digital images in both high- and low-resolution formats

Your photos can be used in many ways. But there are two ways you need to be most concerned with: in print and on the Web. So let your media connections know you have digital images available in high- and low-resolution formats.

For use on websites, low-resolution images are needed (usually JPEG files saved at 72 pixels per inch, although that is changing as computer screens and smartphones improve). For reproduction in print, most publications will want a high-resolution image (often saved as a TIF, JPEG or PNG file at 300 dots per inch).

Whether your photos are shot using a digital camera to begin with or they are prints that you scan, find a way to convert your photos to these digital formats. And, to make it easy for media people to access them, make them available for download from a special page on your website.

Press Clippings

It's an amazing thing. Media exposure often leads to more media exposure. Therefore, you want editors and writers to see what other media have already written about you. Plus, you want radio people and nightclub owners to know what kind of exposure you're getting. The best way to let them know about the growing buzz over your music is through a collection of press clippings.

Here are three things to keep in mind when compiling your press clippings for a physical promo kit:

25) Use photocopies

Don't make the mistake of sending pages (sometimes called "tear sheets") from the original publications that your write-ups appeared in. Instead, make attractive photocopies of those write-ups. For one thing, it can be difficult and expensive to get enough of the original publications to send to everyone on your media list. Most importantly, editors won't be any more impressed by the original than they will by a copy.

Also, basic black and white copies will do just fine. There's no need to print your press clippings in color, unless you have one or two pages that are particularly striking – and you can justify the extra cost to send color copies to prime media contacts.

26) Arrange your clippings neatly on each page

Every time you get reviewed or featured in the press, take the issue and cut out the section in which your piece appears. If it fits on a standard 8.5" x 11" sheet, great. If not, find a print shop with a good photocopier and reduce or enlarge the section to fit nicely on a page.

It's also a good idea to take the publication's logo and name from the front cover and place it on the same page along with the date of the issue. This obviously lets people know the origin of each write-up.

And when you have a few shorter blurbs on your band that aren't substantial enough for their own page, combine them all on one sheet. Just make sure they are all properly labeled by publication and date.

27) Staple your press clipping sheets together

While you want to keep your bio, press release and cover letter as loose sheets, all of your press clippings should be stapled together. Especially if you have a lot of clippings, this makes it easier for the recipient to flip through them without having to juggle reams of loose paper.

Note: With online press kits, you can post short excerpts from reviews and then link to the full-length articles, if they're available online.

Positive Quotes Page

As we already discussed, a media person will rarely listen to your album all the way through – especially the first time. The same goes for reading all of the articles and reviews included in your press clippings. That's where the Positive Quotes Page comes into play. Use these two tips to create yours:

28) Pull out highlights from published reviews

You know that sprinkled throughout all of the write-ups you've earned are some golden nuggets of praise. I suggest you do what major motion picture marketers do: Pull out the best one- or two-sentence quotes from a variety of media sources, as in "'Two thumbs up!' –Roger Ebert." Go through all of the published write-ups in your collection of press clippings and find the most sparkling endorsements.

Examples: "Acme Rock Band sizzles on its debut album!" –*The Podunk Gazette*

"The new disc from Acme Rock Band is chock full of catchy, three-minute pop gems." –*New Music Dispatch*

Take these quotes and display them all on a single sheet or web page. You might put a headline at the top that reads: "Here's what the media are saying about Acme Rock Band ..."

I also suggest using this positive quotes sheet as the cover page for your stapled collection of press clippings. That way, someone could get a quick overview of the great things media sources have been saying about you. And the full-length articles are in the same package for those who want to read a little deeper.

29) Ask select industry people for a comment to include in your kit

What if you're just starting out or have a newly formed band? You may not have many (or any) positive quotes or press clippings. Now what?

Approach people you know in the music business (bloggers, nightclub owners, studio engineers, disc jockeys) and ask them for a comment you can use. "I can always count on The Porcupines to put on a great show at my club!" –Ted Smith, owner, the Cool Club. That's a good start when you're short on traditional media quotes.

Also, when gathering these blurbs, feel free to suggest the wording for the person's comment. He or she can always change or tweak it, but you may be surprised by how many people will accept the blurb you wrote as is and let you use it on your Positive Quotes Page.

Bottom line: You now have the recipe (29 ingredients, to be exact) for cooking up a sizzling music press kit. It's time to go out there and grab your fair share of publicity!

Chapter 11

How to Exploit the Music Media and Get the Widespread Coverage You Deserve

Let's begin this chapter with some good news and bad news. First, the good news:

When it comes to getting exposure through music magazines, newspapers, radio shows, websites, blogs, and podcasts ... there is no shortage of opportunity. There are literally hundreds of thousands (if not millions) of music news sources in existence. From *Rolling Stone* and *Billboard* magazine to small blogs and websites run my amateur journalists – and everything in between.

And most of these sources are hungry for fresh content. They have space to fill with reviews, airtime to fill with songs, pages to fill with interviews, and bandwidth to fill with music videos. There is a limitless need for new music, hot topics, and fresh approaches in style.

Now for the bad news ...

Most independent songwriters, musicians and bands get only a small fraction of the media exposure they deserve. Of course, that sad fact isn't the result of a lack of opportunity. I believe most artists miss out on publicity for two primary reasons:

1) They simply don't take action to pursue media exposure. Whether it's because of distractions or a lack of knowledge, many self-promoting musicians just don't make the effort to contact bloggers, editors, and journalists. And as a result, little publicity comes their way.

2) When they do take action, they approach media people the wrong way. As I mentioned in the previous chapter, I learned a lot about these mistakes during the 10 years I ran my own music magazine. Even though artists and would-be publicists have good intentions, most PR efforts are ineffective and produce few results. With the advice in this and other chapters, I hope to change your fate in this area.

The really sad thing for me is seeing all of the new artists with talent and potential who are either blinded by ignorance or jaded by a lack of progress. These artists soon get comfortable living in the obscurity of what I call "Media Limbo." Which means thousands of music fans never hear about the great musical stuff they have to offer.

Don't Make This Same Mistake!

There are many ways to get the media exposure you want. But first you have to leap over a few hurdles that are currently keeping you from getting to that enviable position.

Before we address these topics, I must point out that this chapter does not cover who to contact. There are many excellent music directories available to help you gather names and addresses. (Plus, you can find names and contact information for practically anybody using this little thing called Google.) What we deal with in this chapter is *how* you go about contacting the media.

Key question: What good is having a hot list of music bloggers and magazine editors if the approach you take to reach them does more harm than good? That's the problem we're going to overcome in the following pages.

So let's start off with one of the biggest mistakes you're probably making right now:

You're not sending messages that inspire media people to act

Having been involved in music for more than a couple of decades now, I can tell you without hesitation that most music marketing communications – fliers, bios, cover letters, websites, email messages, ads and more – are weak and ineffective.

That is, they don't perform the primary function of marketing communication: Getting the person who receives your message to *do something* – call you, email you, listen to your songs, or come to your event. At the very least, the message should pave the way for your follow-up email or phone call at a later date.

Bottom line: Simply getting your stuff in the mail (physically or electronically) is not your ultimate goal. That's where most music marketers go wrong; they throw useless information into the world and hope it sticks on something.

But that's not how you'll be dealing with the media from now on, because now you know that it's your job to send messages that grab attention and motivate the people receiving them to act!

Clarification: I should point out that not every communication with another human being should be motivated by some action you want them to take. There are times when sending a simple email to compliment someone or introduce yourself is all that's needed to plant an initial seed.

There's a time and place for messages that simply make a connection or create awareness. But most musicians stay stuck in this passive mode, not wanting to bother anyone or appear to be pushy.

I'm not suggesting that you be overly aggressive. Marketing and seeking publicity are not about strong-arm tactics or hard selling. But to be effective, you must be clear. There's no room for ambiguity. Oftentimes the best thing you can do is come right out and ask people to do something specific.

How to get the best results with your music news message

With all this in mind, allow me to reiterate: The main goal you should have when you design and create a poster, email, artist bio, press release, or advertisement – whether you're sending it to a media person, venue booker, industry pro or fan – is to get the person receiving it to respond. And preferably to respond NOW!

But first you must know what it is you want them to do and then inspire them to do it (in a firm, yet polite and professional manner).

That's why, before you contact anyone in the media, you must ask yourself the following questions:

Who will receive my music news message?

The type of person getting your marketing materials will determine how you motivate him or her to act. Music fans are inspired by the emotion your music creates within them, the identity you represent that they relate to, and the people they'll hang out with at your shows.

Music industry pros (managers, A&R reps, entertainment attorneys), on the other hand, may be more persuaded to act if the potential to make money and earn a better name for themselves is present.

But media people are a different breed. So what motivates them? What would get a music editor, influential blogger, freelance writer, or radio station program director to get excited enough to contact you or cover you right away?

Which leads to the next question ...

How should I persuade media people to take action?

In a nutshell, media people are motivated by these four things:

1) Amusing and entertaining their specific audience. The first duty for a writer, podcaster or radio show host is not to give your music career a boost. It's to do his best job to retain and increase his audience.

2) Being the first one in their region or niche to "break" a new, up-and-coming act. When media types earn the reputation of being on the cutting edge, it makes them feel good. They love to be on top of trends and ahead of the cultural curve.

3) Not missing the boat on something that is generating a buzz. While some editors and program directors like being on the leading edge, others also like to play it safe by turning their readers/listeners (and their paying advertisers) on to something that has already proven itself popular.

4) Exposing something that is witty or creative enough to grab their attention. Many hundreds of acts over the years have inspired the media to action with either a funny band name, unusual album title, or other promotional gimmick. Acts such as KISS, Gwar and Dread Zeppelin come to mind. Do you have a clever gimmick? If you do, just make sure the novelty aspect will create a reputation you can live with for years to come.

What do I want media people to do?

Run-of-the-mill music promoters toss literature about themselves to the media and leave it up to the media person to decide what to do next. But you won't do this. Remember, with few exceptions, the only reason you invest time and money to correspond with someone about your music is to motivate them to act!

Therefore, you will spell out in your email messages and cover letters, in no uncertain terms, what you want the recipients to do. Call, email, come to your gig, listen to your CD, download your MP3, wait for your follow-up call ... whatever it is, ask them politely, yet very specifically, to do it.

Note: That doesn't mean media people will automatically do what you ask – more often than not, they won't. But at least you will have answered that nagging but all-important question: What happens next?

When do I want media people to take action?

Years ago I received a press kit from a musician who wanted me to write about his band. It was similar to hundreds of other packages I've received over the years. The accompanying letter went on and on about what his band had done, how much the musician thought of himself, and that he wanted to appear on the cover of *Spotlight*, the music magazine I published.

(***Warning***: You should never insist on a "cover story" on your band. That's a decision the editor makes based on what's best for the publication, regardless of who enthusiastically asked for it.)

However, nowhere in this guy's letter did it specify what he'd do next to further the process along. In essence, he was saying:

"Here's a bunch of stuff about me and my needs. Now it's your job to figure out what it is I want you to do now to stroke my inflated ego even more. It doesn't matter if I hear from you today, next month or next year, and you may not hear from me ever again. The thing that's most important is that I've given you more material to fill your trash can with!"

Lesson: This craziness must stop! If it seems I'm being hard on this guy, it's only to prove a point: Spell out all of the things you have to offer media people and then kindly give them specific marching orders (in a casual and friendly manner) on what they should do next – or expect from you next – and what they get from you when they do it.

In case your head is spinning from all this advice, here's an example that meets all the requirements of being an effective message you might send to a media person:

Hi Sam,

It's Brad from The New Tones here. You may recall we corresponded a couple months ago after you wrote about the resurgence of vinyl on your blog. I'm a big fan of your work.

Say, I wanted to let you know that my psychedelic jam band will be performing in Springfield on August 18 as part of our Midwest tour. I'd be happy to add you to the guest list that night.

It would be so great to meet you in person while we are in town. And if you feel that a preview write-up on your blog would be appropriate, I'd be happy to supply you with whatever you need to make that happen.

Two things your readers might be interested in:

1) We are releasing a limited edition vinyl version of our new album, called Needle to the Groove. (The Jam Band Gazette rated it one of the "top three releases of the year.")

2) We are touring with a string section – two violinists and a cello player. How many indie jam bands can claim that?

Below is a link to our EPK. If you would like me to send you a physical CD or vinyl record, just reply to this email and say so. I'll get one out to you right away.

I'll touch base again next week if I don't hear from you. Cheers!

Brad

Hopefully, you can see that this message is direct and positive. It keeps the needs of the journalist and his audience in mind. It's relevant and not totally centered on the band and its need for publicity. It asks for a response, while also letting the blogger know what will happen next.

That's what effective music publicity tactics are all about!

Chapter 12

5 Steps to Getting an Avalanche of Media Exposure

You want free publicity, right? Great. I want to help you get more of it. So far in this section we've covered press kits, what media people really want, clever ways to stand out, and more. To cap things off, here are the five steps you can take to turn yourself into a music publicity power house and get a ton of free exposure.

Ready? Let's dig in.

1) Identify your top media sources

A lot of musicians are attracted to the notion of getting publicity. They like the idea of getting their name "out there." I'm sure you do too. But to be truly effective, you must clarify the type of publicity you want and clearly define where "out there" you want your name to go.

So the first step to getting a lot of media exposure is to identify what publicity and music news sources you want to target. Sorry, but "whatever I can get" or "everywhere" doesn't cut it. You must get specific and actually compile a media "hit list" that you plan to contact.

What forms of media would you like exposure on? Blogs? Online radio shows? Print publications? TV shows? You really need to decide. Also note that for each general category of media, you can define it further by whether it is local, regional, national, or international in scope.

Advice: It's fine to go after sources that cover a variety of music or that seem to be indie artist friendly, but your best bet is to find and focus on media that cover your specific sub-genre. Targeting a general jazz publication is good, but if you uncover a site or writer who specializes in Afro-Cuban music (and you play Afro-Cuban jazz), that would be even better.

In other words, narrowcast your search for the ideal music media sources. Especially if you're just starting out or trying to promote a new artist, start your list with smaller niche bloggers and local journalists. Then widen the net to include more general and indie friendly sites, along with sources that tie into other aspects of your identity. Only then should you move up the food chain and approach more prominent publications and editors.

2) Make an introductory connection

I see a certain mistake made by eager music marketers all the time. And sometimes it just can't be helped. In fact, I've made this mistake myself when I had an event or new book that I needed to promote now. I had identified my media hit list, so I started reaching out to get publicity.

You've probably done the same thing. But there's a better way.

The problem with this "ready, aim, fire" approach is that the journalist is often hearing from you for the very first time when you have a debut album or big event you are trying to promote now. A more effective strategy would have you planting seeds long before you have something to promote.

That's why I recommend some advance planning. And that's why coming up with a list of media sources ahead of time can be so helpful. It allows you time to reach out and introduce yourself long before you are on deadline and need to ask for something.

Strategy: Every time you come across a blog, radio show, or publication that seems ideal for your type of music, do these two things:

- Add the source to your database of media contacts; and ...

- Send the writer or show host a quick email saying how much you enjoyed a specific article or recent episode. Make this note personal and specific, and don't ask for anything. But do include a brief description of your music in the "signature file" of your email, along with links to your website and social media profiles.

Taking these important early steps will help warm up the music journalists you target and will pave the way for a mountain of publicity in the near future.

3) Choose your publicity angle for each source

Now that you've identified your ideal media sources and have made an introductory connection with them, it's time to get busy asking for coverage, right?

Wrong!

There's one more important step you'll need to take before you start pitching yourself to the media. This step answers that all-important question:

What are you going to say to each media contact when you email or call them?

Sorry, but "Hey, I want some free press for my band's new album" is not the right answer. You must put some thought into what comes out of your mouth or what emanates from your fingertips in an email.

I know I've already covered this concept, but it's so essential I want to stress it again: Stop talking so much about yourself in "I-Me-My" terms. Most band bios, cover letters, and email messages are littered with "I am ... We want ... I think this ... We did that ... I, I, I ..."

Perhaps you're not clear about why this is important. You may be asking, "How else am *I* supposed to tell media people about *me* and *my* music?"

The answer: By focusing on what's in it for the media person! (If you're not sure what that is, review the four points in the previous chapter.) The problem with all of this "me"-centered marketing is that it is usually void of the most important marketing word of all: "You."

Let's face it. Most people are motivated by some level of self-interest; they naturally focus on themselves. It's probably an ancient human survival instinct left over from the caveman era. And that's fine. It's not a crime to put a priority on your goals and aspirations. But when you communicate with others, it's important to resist the urge to focus on yourself.

As I've stressed in other sections of this book, to get what you want, you must cater to other people's goals and aspirations. You have to figure out how your needs can be met by helping others meet their own desires.

From now on, I'd like you to keep in mind that what motivates media people (and all people, for that matter) is what they get out of various relationships. Whenever you communicate with someone – whether on the Internet, in person, on the phone, or in writing – he or she is either consciously or unconsciously asking, "So what's in this for me, bub?"

Your job is to answer that unspoken question and deliver something of value. So before you make a connection with media people, determine what your benefit-oriented angle is. Why would your story and music be of interest to the readers, listeners, or viewers of this blog, show or publication?

Can you find an interesting angle beyond "we have a new album out." Thousands of new albums come out every week. You have every right to be excited about yours, but the simple fact that you just released one is not "news." So dig deeper for an interesting hook that ties into a current event or something the publication has covered before. Is there anything unusual about your project, a band member, or a theme that runs throughout your music?

Also, the PR angle you use with one publication can be different from the angle you use with another. It's important to find the overlap between the theme of the media source and some aspect of you and your music.

Bottom line: When you know your publicity angle before you contact media people, your odds of success are greatly enhanced.

This topic of publicity angles (also called "news hooks" and "story ideas") is a big one. I only scratch the surface here. I cover this subject in much greater detail in my program *Music Publicity Insider's Guide*. Visit www.TheBuzzFactor.com for details.

4) Pitch your story

Okay. Now that you know your publicity angle and what you're going to say, it's time to reach out and say it. There are all sorts of ways to contact the media and deliver your messages to them. You can send physical press kits with cover letters to dozens of sources at the same time, or you could bulk email the same pitch to several publications at once.

But, I have a feeling you know that wouldn't be the most effective way to go about it. The best method is the personal, one-on-one approach. That means, one by one, you craft a short email or make a quick phone call to each person on your media hit list.

And, as you do this, direct your message to what you intelligently guess are the media person's hot buttons. Therefore, when communicating with a member of the media, don't write something like this:

My name is Jake and I play in a band called the Blazing Scots. We just released our new album and it is really good. I would love to get some exposure on your blog. We could really use it.

The most common response to this type of marketing is: "So what? Who cares what you could use? Why should I add to my already busy schedule to help you?"

But what if, instead, you tried this approach with the next email you sent?

Come on, admit it. When was the last time you heard bagpipes in a local rock venue? Probably never. But that's what you'll hear and see when the Blazing Scots come to Atlanta next month – October 10 at the XTC Club.

This will be our first time performing in Atlanta. From what I've seen of your column, your readers will dig the Blazing Scots as we pour our Angus infused heritage into a two-hour marathon of lusty bagpipe magic.

(Love the piece you did last month on thrift store rock stars, by the way. Hilarious!)

You should receive our CD and press kit in the mail by Friday. I'll follow up with a phone call next week to see if there's anything else you need to let your people know about the October 10 show.

If you're interested in attending as my guest, say the word and I'll be sure to put you on the guest list. Cheers!

Notice the difference?

Hopefully you can see how "you"-oriented this second message is and how much more effective it could be than the example before it. There's also a real "news" hook spelled out in the text: The band's first show in Atlanta and something unusual (bagpipes) at a rock club.

Lesson: It's the same band and the same information, just a better way to present it to get results. The former pile of ... um, words ... is ego-driven and bland. The latter speaks directly to the media person and what's in it for her. It addresses her needs, not yours. And it does so in a fun and inviting way.

Are you starting to get the picture?

I've taken up a good amount of space to address this issue of placing your primary focus on a benefit to the other person. It's a crucial perspective that will make a world of difference to your music career.

So heed this advice and put it to good use!

5) Follow up ... always!

Question: Do you follow through on your music publicity efforts? Before you give me a knee-jerk "Yes" answer, really think about it. Honestly. When you send a press kit, leave a voice mail message, or send an email to a media person, do you contact that person again if you don't get a response within a few days?

Do you equate the silence you get after a single attempt to reach someone as a big, fat "No" – and then curse the world because no one seems to give a rat's buttocks about you? Don't stress. Just pick up the phone or fire off another email. You may be surprised by the immense progress you make just by doing this one simple thing.

Case in point: Several years ago I wanted to get some publicity by tapping into the popularity of the TV talent show *American Idol*. I decided to take a controversial stand and wrote a press release with the headline "What's Wrong with American Idol?" My news hook was that the show does a disservice to the public by painting an unrealistic picture of how music careers are built in this digital, do-it-yourself era.

Great. So I eagerly shot off a few emails pitching the story to some local St. Louis media people I knew. Then every couple of hours I checked my inbox for a response. After a few days, guess how many replies I got.

Zilch.

Not one person got back to me. And these were people I actually knew and had relationships with. Sheesh! I admit it, I thought the idea was so clever and timely that people would get in line to interview me. But it didn't happen.

I could have sulked and given up. Instead, I did something that the majority of music promoters never do: I sent follow-up emails to all of them. And this time the results were quite different.

Within a couple of hours, the first reply came from a radio talk show host. "Sorry, but I'm gonna pass for now." It was disappointing, but at least I got a response.

Later that day, a second reply came from a radio news show producer. "Sorry I didn't reply sooner. I like this idea a lot. Can you do a ten-minute phone interview next Sunday?" Now we were getting somewhere.

The next day I really hit the follow-up jackpot. After a TV reporter for the CBS affiliate read my second email more closely, he loved the idea. I was immediately booked to appear on his weekend TV news show. In addition, a week later I was a guest on his morning talk-radio show.

All of this came to me because I took the time to follow up. I've seen this same pattern play out time and time again, whether it was seeking publicity, booking gigs, or making sales offers to my mailing list. The follow up is where the real payoff is!

The thing is, most music promoters don't connect a second or third time with people they try to reach. To average marketers, a lack of response must mean a lack of interest – that the artist or story idea isn't worthy. But that isn't always the case.

People are busy. They may be interested in your proposal but get sidetracked and forget about you. Not to worry. A friendly reminder note can be just the thing to reawaken their intentions to get back to you. Or it can be the trigger that inspires them to more seriously consider your idea and make a decision on it.

The difference between success and failure can often be measured in mere inches. Following up is just one way you can set yourself apart and make people wonder how you got so lucky to enjoy all the exposure that seems to naturally come your way.

There you go. Now you have five steps you can implement right now to get more media exposure.

Key question: What happens now? Will you remain part of the majority of music marketers – people who say they really want to pursue music press coverage on a wider scale … but never get past talking about it?

Or, will you be part of the top two percent of the music community – people who understand the difference between "knowing" things and "doing" things?

Ask the most prosperous artists. They'll tell you that being successful means taking that burning belief in yourself, mixing it with education and timely information, then adding in a healthy dose of action.

Are you that type of person? I sincerely hope so.

Now that you're armed with guerrilla music marketing basics, Internet promotion savvy, and publicity know-how, it's time to start learning about how to make money with all the buzz you create. That's what we cover in the next section.

Section 4:
Guerrilla Music
Money & Sales

Chapter 13

32 Ways to Sell a Lot More of Your CDs, Downloads and Music Merchandise

You've put a lot of time and effort into writing good original songs and committing them to finished tracks in the studio. You crafted the artwork and packaging, and you arranged for your album to finally be manufactured and made available for download.

Many musicians describe the feeling of seeing their slickly packaged final creation for the first time: It's a wonderful sensation of accomplishment. They feel like shouting at the top of their lungs to let the world know about this great thing they've got to offer.

That's why it pains me to see so many music makers drop the ball at this point. Sure, they say they want to get recognition from lots of people who have been touched by their music. And, let's face it, they wouldn't mind making a bit of money selling their product too.

So why do artists continue to manufacture 1,000 CDs only to have 900 of them sit in a closet and gather dust?

The simple answer: These artists haven't learned effective methods for marketing their recordings and merchandise. Also, they haven't done their homework and haven't discovered the many resources available to help them sell their music. Are you one of these people? If so, don't worry. There's help within the pages ahead.

What follows are 32 solid ideas and resources to expand your thinking and help you sell more of your independent releases and related products.

1) Get committed

Not to an asylum, but to becoming an independent music marketer – instead of just a music producer. Unless you're simply making music for your immediate friends and family (which is worthy in itself), you're going to have to expand your skills to include more than songwriting and recording techniques.

Far too many musically creative people feel that if they just come up with great music, the world will beat a path to their door. While this approach might work for a select few, most songwriters and musicians have to take a few extra steps to get their music noticed and bought in bulk by enthusiastic fans.

Important: The first step in your efforts to sell more of your music and merchandise is to make a decision right now. Are you willing to spend as much time and energy marketing your musical pride and joy as you do creating it? This means you are eager to indulge in the art of researching your market, networking with people who can help you accomplish your sales goals and, ultimately, becoming as inspired by exposing your music as you are by playing it.

Are you truly ready for this? You'll need to be if you want to boost your music sales and income.

2) Know who your fans are and why they buy

Yes, this is covered in another chapter, but let's emphasize it again: How would you describe the ideal consumer of your music? And what inspires him or her to buy your music and merchandise? If you can't answer these questions, you may have a tough battle (not to mention a closet full of CDs) ahead of you.

Acts that develop a loyal fan base usually have a specific musical focus and image that their fans identify with so strongly, they pack the group's shows and buy tons of their stuff. The magnet that draws these fans is the personality of the band, combined with a sound, look and vibe that supports it.

Get a handle on what attitude, sound and image you portray – and how those things positively affect the way your fans feel. Knowing this will help you position your act for maximum exposure … and sales!

Important note: Make sure the image you promote is a true part of who you are. Copping an identity only because you think it will sell will get you nowhere fast.

3) If you perform live at all, have physical CDs to sell

I know. As consumers get more comfortable with digital music and media, many artists are selling fewer CDs. This leads many artists to wonder if they even need to make physical copies of their music available at all. Here's my best advice: If you perform live with any regularity at all, YES!

You should have physical products on hand and offer them for sale. They can be full-length CDs or shorter EPs with only five or six songs on them; or perhaps a USB drive filled with many music and video files. Whatever shape it takes, do make your recorded music available in a form that a fan can carry out of the venue. Simply sending fans to your website or iTunes to buy music and expecting them to actually do that is risky. Even people who genuinely intend to do so will forget and get sidetracked. Many artists have tried to sell download cards at gigs with mixed results.

Your best bet is still to have some type of CD with at least minimal packaging and artwork – something that can be autographed and handed to a fan. Especially if you make special sales offers at your live shows that are only good that night, you will inspire sales (and cash flow).

With this in mind, note that several of the proceeding tips will reference physical CDs. However, keep in mind that most of these marketing principles can be applied to digital sales as well.

4) Create new music sales categories

You can add real marketing muscle to your releases if you can develop a fresh approach to defining them. New Age music, for instance, is often marketed through spiritual "rock shops" as a sonic stimulus people can use to relax, meditate and unwind. Some record labels have thematic releases that are packaged with books on the same subject, which opens up bookstore sales and other methods of distribution.

Another example: Years ago a Memphis, TN-based company called Hands On Inc. promoted Driving Music. It was a self-created category of music specially recorded and mastered for car audio systems. The clever people behind this concept said the process, which they call "Precision Mastering," makes the best use of the peculiar acoustic environment of the automobile – without needing extra equipment.

Added advantage: By creating this new category, Hands On Inc. also opened up a new retail distribution source: They marketed the releases through auto centers.

Can you think of a fresh distribution channel that would work for you?

5) Package your releases as a related series

Jazz musician Cole Broderick came up with the idea to produce a series of four albums based on the changing seasons of Saratogo Springs, NY, where he spends a good deal of his time. The first release in the series, the aptly titled *Springtime in Saratoga*, was followed up with releases relating to summer, autumn and winter. What a great concept.

Packaging a series of related titles brings with it a lot of advantages:

- **It encourages repeat buying.** Music fans who purchase one in the series will be more inclined to get the entire set – if they like what they hear on the first one, of course.

- **Distributors and retailers love it.** They know they'll have more than one product coming from you. Plus they realize each release encourages more sales of the others.

- **It makes for a great media hook.** This unique approach to your music makes you stand out when editors and writers are making story decisions.

Consider the series method when planning your future recording projects.

6) Make the most of sales opportunities at live shows

Hands down, live shows are one of your best ways to promote a new release and sell merchandise. However, many musicians think it's uncool to repeatedly plug their "product" at gigs.

Reality: You want people to come to your shows because they like your music, right? If they've taken the time to set aside an evening to experience your live show, wouldn't many of them also want to take your recorded music home? Of course. Don't deny them that experience. And don't deny yourself the monetary rewards of selling more of your music.

Live shows create the perfect buying environment. People in the audience experience your music and personality firsthand. You touch them in the most direct way. At the same time, a busy club or concert hall can have a lot of distractions. That's why you need to be somewhat assertive and hawk your wares regularly from the stage, as long as you do it in a cool and confident way.

7) Print and distribute a mini-newsletter

Many artists pass out fliers or calendars of upcoming shows at their live gigs. It's not a bad idea, but fliers get tossed in the trash pretty quickly and usually won't help your overall efforts to sell more music and merchandise. One solution may be to publish a mini-newsletter that's filled with tidbits of information on your band along with a list of items you have for sale.

I also advocate publishing an email newsletter, but this section specifically refers to a short paper newsletter you hand out at shows. This idea might seem "old school" in a digital world at first glance. But I think it has some merit if used correctly. If you rely on people accessing your info only on their phones, tablets or computers, you may be limiting the ways your fans are reminded of you.

Clarification: When I suggest a mini-newsletter I'm talking about a single sheet of paper that is printed on both sides. Yes, it should contain links to your website and social media profiles. And to help you sell more music and merchandise, it should also list some of the things you have for sale. But to make sure people take it with them and hang onto it, this mini-newsletter should also feature something funny, helpful or intriguing too.

Perhaps you could include some interesting details about the band members, or a list of the ten best albums or independent artists in your genre. Another idea you might try is to list several trivia questions related to your style of music, then have fans go to a page on your website to uncover the answers. Of course, that web page should also direct people to a special offer to buy your music (or get on your mailing list) while they are there.

8) Capture new fans through the media

As you know, a great way to build up a following is to compile and use a mailing list. (You do have one, don't you?) Make no mistake, your mailing list can be a powerful tool in stimulating sales. But live gigs and your website are not the only places to collect these lucrative names and addresses.

When you do media interviews, you're reaching perhaps thousands of potential fans (and buyers). Make the best use of that opportunity by offering something of value to readers, listeners or viewers – free downloads, a sticker, band comic book, novelty condom ... anything to inspire music fans to connect with you. You can have people go to your website, send you a text message, or call the station while you're on the air.

Bottom line: Give fans a reason to connect with you and hand over their contact info in exchange for your cool freebie.

9) Use the two-step approach when you run paid ads

I want to preface this section by making it clear that I don't advocate paying for ads, especially if it's early in an artist's career or it's motivated by a misguided notion that throwing money at obscurity is the way to build a fan base. It's not. After all, this is the "guerrilla" guide to music marketing on a budget.

However, there are times when running some paid ads makes sense or is worth experimenting with. But when you do, it's usually a mistake to expect your advertising to generate many direct sales. That might work for Coldplay or U2, since they each have a long history and an established fan base. But people will rarely buy music right away from an independent artist they are not that familiar with (refer back to the three steps in Chapter 1 for more clarity on this).

The most effective tactic with paid ads is to use what has classically been called the "two-step advertising" approach. That means you use your ads to "generate leads." In musician terms, that means you promote something that a music fan can get for free. That special something you give away should ideally be of interest to a very specific type of fan. And, to get this freebie, fans simply need to enter their name and email address.

Lesson: This strategy gives you more control over the marketing process. Most artists and record labels simply throw their name out into the public. Then they hope and pray someone will take notice and be intrigued enough to drop everything else they're doing, hop in the car or surf to their website, and purchase their album. I ask you: What percentage of people interested in your ad are really going to do that?

Therefore, you – being the creative music promoter that you are – won't take that roll-of-the-dice approach. From now on, you'll take control and gather the names and addresses of people who are interested in your style of music. And you'll gather those details by offering potential fans something free in exchange for handing over their personal contact information.

Once you have this vital fan contact information, you have the power to gently remind and directly inspire them – through your regular follow-up communications – to take the next logical step: buying your music or other piece of merchandise.

Key insight: Don't be a victim of chance when it comes to your music promotion. Grab the reigns and take control of the process!

10) Offer radio stations free copies to give away

Media folks love to give away stuff to their audiences. So don't be shy about asking your local college and community stations if they'd give away your new CD on the air. Of course, you should also offer to come in, do an interview, and play tracks off the album (or perform live) to tie in with the giveaway.

And be sure to let listeners know where they can go (online and off) to purchase your album. Radio exposure of any kind can be good for your notoriety and the sales of your recorded music.

11) Give copies to retail stores for in-store play

This may seem obvious, but a lot of musicians overlook this important marketing technique. A retail store that sells music is the perfect place to capture the attention of music fans. And it doesn't have to be a traditional "record store" (which is harder to find these days anyway). Any retail outlet that might attract your ideal type of fan is fair game.

Insight: Customers who visit these establishments are already in a buying mood and environment. Even if they came into the store in search of clothes or furniture, they might very well be enticed to buy music if they hear something they like.

Ask any store clerk how many times customers come up and ask, "Who is that playing over the speakers right now?" Meet with store managers, make arrangements for them to sell your CDs, and give them free promotional copies to play while customers are shopping.

12) Set up retail store appearances, autograph sessions, and unplugged performances

I know what you're thinking: "A store appearance? That would be awfully pompous of me!" Not so fast. The national touring acts aren't the only musicians worthy of such events. Setting up an in-store appearance gives you weeks of exposure in the store in the form of fliers promoting the date. In-store events also get people talking and, in the case of unplugged performances, get your music to the ears of consumers who might never have heard you otherwise. Remember, people have to hear you before they'll buy.

13) Offer local stores a free package-stuffer

Many retail businesses stuff a flier or discount coupon into customers' bags along with their purchases. Wouldn't it be great to get a record store or other retailer to put your small flier into all of its customers' packages? Your message would go directly to the music-buying public!

Print some professionally designed inserts promoting your CD. Visit stores and ask managers to use the inserts. You might find sympathetic owners who will do it simply to help you out. But you'll quite likely meet resistance with this unusual request. What then? Call it quits? Hardly.

Hot tip: Make the package insert two-sided. Offer to put the store's message on one side and your message on the other. You pay for printing the whole thing. That way, the store gets free promotion and an incentive to stuff them – and you get lots of direct exposure for very little cost.

14) Find alternate ways to market your music

Is there a non-music publication or offbeat hobby that fans of your musical style might be interested in? If so, you might consider reaching potential new fans through these unlikely means.

Example: Years ago BMG moved a lot of hard rock and metal sampler CDs by advertising them through, of all things, comic books. The albums featured cuts from such bands as 21 Guns, Babylon AD and the Rollins Band. Readers could order the samplers via a toll-free 800 number.

"There is a significant portion of the comic-reading and record-buying public that overlaps," said a VP of marketing at BMG. A number of the comic book respondents bought full albums based on hearing tracks on the sampler – and that's exactly what BMG wanted.

How can you do something similar with your music on a smaller scale?

15) Create incentives to buy

There are a number of effective ways to make offers that will inspire additional sales. The trick is to dangle more alluring benefits in front of them while their interest level is running high. This isn't being manipulative, by the way. You're simply giving people an opportunity to get more of the great musical stuff they already enjoy.

Example: Let's say someone buys your band's latest CD by mail. The average music marketer would stick the album in a package and send it off. Period. Maybe later, he or she might send a post card or email featuring other merchandise. But why wait?

Better: The smart Guerrilla Music Marketer sends the CD along with a flier listing all available products (past releases, T-shirts, caps, posters, even CDs by other comparable bands). In addition, the package would include a certificate stating something along the lines of:

"Thanks for your order. To show our appreciation, please use this 10 percent-off coupon on your next purchase of band merchandise. As an added bonus, order within the next 30 days and take an entire 20 percent off. It's our way of saying thanks for supporting our music."

See how this works? You can do the same thing using email or your website.

16) Create a catalog or website of similar artists

Contact other similarly styled bands in your region that have albums available. Pool your resources and print a low-cost catalog featuring all of the bands' albums (or create a flier that directs people to a website that serves the same purpose). Hand out the catalogs at your gigs and promote them to the media.

A catalog or website of several artists sharing the same theme carries a lot more weight with both fans and the media than a flier selling your products alone. Use this hook to build your mailing list and sell more of your own releases – while helping other bands in your region.

17) Produce sampler CDs as a promotional tool

People need to hear your music before they can decide if they like it enough to buy your album. Getting enough radio airplay to sufficiently expose your music can be a challenge. Sampler CDs are one solution. Take two or three songs from your full-length album and put them on a sampler CD. Ask retail stores to give them away. Use them as a freebie for people who sign up on your mailing list at gigs. Send a press release to the media announcing that the CDs are available to anyone by mail for two or three dollars to cover shipping.

18) Make a John Hancock offer

When you make a new CD release available, offer a limited number of autographed copies … but only to the first 25 or 50 people who order. My best advice: Keep the promised number of signed copies small. This will inspire serious fans to order even faster. Of course, you can actually deliver more autograph copies than you promised. But by making it a limited offer, fans will be more motivated to send money your way now.

(By the way, John Hancock was the signer with the largest signature on the U.S. *Declaration of Independence*.)

19) Use a point-of-purchase display

Looking for a professional way to display your CDs in stores and on your merch table at live shows? Make use of cardboard countertop displays. Ask record store employees if they have displays they don't need any more. Fix them up and decorate them with your artwork.

If you want to purchase brand-new displays, check out the following companies:

Disc Makers
www.discmakers.com (search for Countertop Display)

CD Stands
www.cdstands.com

Counter Displays
www.counterdisplay.com

Cactus Containers
www.cactuscontainers.com (look for Counter-Top Displays)

20) Get on bestseller, most popular, and most downloaded lists

True music fans hate to miss out on the latest craze within their preferred genre. One of the ways fans discover what's hot is by looking over the growing number of popularity lists on various music websites. These lists come in all shapes and sizes: Top Sellers, Most Listened To, Most Popular Downloads, etc. The higher your ranking on these lists, the more attention you draw to yourself ... and the more sales you can potentially make.

So how can you get visibility on these lists? Well, writing and recording a fantastic song and getting it out there is the first step. An audience will find a killer song through word of mouth alone. But you can help things along by asking your fans and friends to visit, vote, download, listen or whatever it takes to help you rank higher on these lists.

Suggestion: Pick one such list on one site in a category where you feel pretty confident you can make an impact. Ask the people on your mailing list to visit that site and take the required action on the same day or during the same week. This concentrated effort may be all it takes to get you to move higher on the list, where other fans who don't know about you yet will discover you.

21) Make compelling offers and ask for the sale

Some people make a purchase right away when something interests them. Some rarely make a purchase. And a lot of people teeter on the fence, not sure which direction to go. For this third group of good folks, you need to create incentives – reasons for them to hit the Buy button now.

Here are some compelling possibilities:

- **Limited-time discounts**: Get a 20 percent discount if you purchase by this Friday.

- **Limited-quantity offers**: The first 25 people who order get an autographed copy or a bonus download.

- **Upsell with a special offer**: Buy two CDs, get a third one free. Or buy our new album, get our previous release at half off.

- **Bundling**: Purchase a CD, T-shirt and cap at the same time, and save 50 percent.

- **Charity benefit**: 20 percent of all music and merchandise sales proceeds go to the local Wildlife Refuge.

22) Boost CD sales without lowering your price

Here's a great tip from New Zealand musician Mike Barry:

"My band played a festival recently and had our CDs at the merchandise table along with two other bands," Mike writes, "but none of us was selling any." All three bands had their CDs on sale for $10 each. "Out of desperation, I made three piles of CDs and created a sign that read 'Festival Special! 3 CDs for $30.'"

The result: "We sold all three piles in 10 minutes! So we made three more piles and sold them in 10 minutes too. Before we knew it, there was a small crowd around the table. Just the thought of three CDs for $30 sounded too good to pass up. But what's funny is, that is how much it would have cost if the fans bought one off each of us to start with. Amazing!"

Mike's story reminds me of a lesson I learned at a retail store job I had when I was a teenager. I remember a manager one time bragging about how he took some item that normally sold for 39 cents each and sold out of them by displaying them with a sign that announced "2 for a dollar."

Yes, the store sold more of them at a higher price. Why? Because the sign and display created a perception of value. Think about that ... and use this knowledge to sell more of your music and merchandise.

23) Sell an identity with your T-shirts and merchandise

I've seen artists make this mistake hundreds of times. They are so eager to increase music and merchandise sales. They invest in a quality recording and album artwork, and then they have a line of T-shirts, caps and beer koozies printed and ready to sell.

But they are often disappointed that so few T-shirts and other merch items actually move. So what's the problem?

Most of the time, the artist's merchandise has his name and logo printed on them – and that's it. The artwork is well done, but the only thing that makes them unique is the artist's name.

Reality: That might be a sensible thing to do if you're a well-established artist with a hardcore fan base. But when you're a new artist who is building momentum, your fans are still getting to know you. Most of them are not going to be motivated to wear something that professes their love for you ... at least not yet.

However, your small group of early fans may very well be motivated to purchase something from you that reinforces an idea they already have of themselves.

Consider some of the T-shirt designs that the band The Ready Set has made available. "Feel Good Now" is the title of one of their albums. But it also happens to be an idea that many people find appealing. So the band members printed the album title in large letters on their T-shirts. They smartly knew that fans would be attracted to the "Feel Good Now" sentiment.

The Ready Set has another shirt with the words "Pop Music Is a Disease, Get Tested" emblazoned on it. That's a slogan that allows fans to profess their love for an entire genre, not just the band, and do it with an edgy vibe.

Oddly enough, "the ready set" band name sits in smaller letters on the shirts below each of the larger slogans above. The shirts don't focus on the band name; they zero in on a lifestyle and attitude.

The band Shut Up and Deal does something similar with its T-shirt that proclaims, "American Pop Punk, Shut Up and Deal." Again, the shirt is promoting the genre, and the band name itself just happens to be a phrase that reinforces an attitude that the musicians and their fans share. Nice!

Yes, people buy music and merchandise from artists they "like." And yes, many fans will take pleasure in supporting you and playing a role in your growth.

Key point: But what's the deeper reason that most fans spend money on you – especially when it comes to T-shirts and other wearable items? I mentioned it earlier, but it's worth repeating: People buy and wear things that reinforce an image they have of themselves or an image they aspire to portray.

Humans express who they are (or who they want to be) in all sorts of ways – the cars they drive, the stores they shop at, the clothes they wear, the music they listen to, etc. Your job is to create merchandise that helps your fans express who they are – not just sell them stuff with your name and logo on it!

Resources for Music Sales and Distribution

There are a growing number of websites and services that will help you distribute and sell your independent music online. The following companies do not comprise a complete list. But, as of this writing, they represent what I feel are the top sites and services to consider for music sales.

24) CD Baby
www.cdbaby.com

No discussion of online music promotion and sales would be complete without talking about CD Baby. It's the #1 indie music sales site in the world. Since 1998, the site has sold several million physical CDs online to customers and paid more than $250 million directly to artists. If you have an album for sale, you need to make it available there.

In addition, the service allows artists to sell downloads from the CD Baby site as well as on iTunes, Amazon MP3 and others. It can also hook you up to take credit card orders at live gigs, sell or give away download cards, and get plugged into distribution to thousands of music retail stores.

CD Baby founder Derek Sivers sold the company in 2008 to Disc Makers, which has made a lot of improvements to what was already a great service for indie artists. For an overview of what CD Baby currently offers, visit members.cdbaby.com.

25) Tunecore
www.tunecore.com

With physical CD sales continuing to decline and music download sales on the rise, everyone wants to get their music on iTunes, Napster, Emusic, Rhapsody, and other digital music sales sites. The good news is, it's never been easier for independent artists to do just that. One way is to go through CD Baby, covered in the previous tip. Another prominent site that offers this service is Tunecore.

While CD Baby charges few upfront costs to get your music on iTunes and the others, they do take an ongoing percentage as their fee (currently 9% of the net sales). Tunecore uses a different model: They charge an annual subscription to get your songs digitally distributed, and then you keep all the revenue after that.

With both sites you can now register a single song if you want – a great way to go if you have a hot track you want to promote but no full album to go with it.

Note: You can't use both CD Baby and Tunecore for digital distribution. You must choose one service or the other.

26) Amazon.com's Advantage Program
www.amazon.com/advantage

It may not seem to be the music haven that iTunes and CD Baby are, but Amazon gets so much traffic, it shouldn't be ignored. Millions of people visit the site every day, and many go looking for new music, especially at the Amazon MP3 store. So you really should have your music on Amazon.

There are a number of ways to make your music available for sale directly from Amazon. If you use a distributor, they may handle that for you. But you can make the arrangements yourself by joining Amazon's Advantage program.

There's a $29.95 annual program fee (per account, not per album title), and you must be willing to part with 55% of your album's retail price. That's right, you'll end up with 45% of the suggested retail price you set.

Reality check: Many musicians cry foul over the percentage split. But, the truth is, you'd give a traditional distributor a big chunk of the retail price anyway. Amazon serves a similar function, and it reaches millions of online music buyers. So just bite the bullet and make your music available on the site.

Note that when you join the Advantage program, you must ship CDs to Amazon promptly in the amounts they order, which will ramp up or down as each album's sales figures warrant. It's more hands-on than the CreateSpace option I'll cover in a moment, but it's a viable way you should be aware of. You can also make your songs available for sale in the Amazon MP3 store with an Advantage program account.

27) CreateSpace
www.createspace.com

Amazon also runs a company called CreateSpace that produces print-on-demand CDs, DVDs and books for independent artists, record labels, authors, and more. If you're looking for a more "hands off" method of getting your music on Amazon, CreateSpace may be an ideal solution.

According to the site: "Distribute your music on Amazon.com and other sales channels as an audio CD or MP3 download. Set the list price for your audio CDs and choose from a selection of royalty plans for your MP3 downloads. Use our online tools to set up your titles – they're free! Since copies of your titles are manufactured as customers order, you'll never worry about inventory and set-up fees."

28) ReverbNation.com
www.reverbnation.com

ReverbNation is an online music-marketing platform used by more than a million artists, managers, record labels, and venues.

According to the site, the service "provides free and affordable solutions to individual artists and the music industry professionals who support them in the areas of web promotion, fan-relationship management, digital distribution, social-media marketing, direct-to-fan e-commerce, fan-behavior measurement, sentiment tracking, web-site hosting, and concert booking and promotion."

Just about all of the musicians I've talked to who use ReverbNation speak highly of it. If you promote music online, you should have an account there.

29) Bandcamp
www.bandcamp.com

Bandcamp is another site that offers a lot of musician friendly tools to help you sell music and merchandise. The site lists Sufjan Stevens, Amanda Palmer, and Zoë Keating among its artist users and claims to have driven more than $4 million paid transactions that served 44 million downloads to fans.

According to the site, "On Bandcamp, albums outsell tracks 5 to 1 (in the rest of the music buying world, tracks outsell albums 16 to 1). On name-your-price albums, fans pay an average of 50% more than whatever you set as your minimum." No wonder so many artists are happy using this service.

30) Topspin Media
www.topspinmedia.com

This site created a lot of buzz in recent years as a new direct-to-fan platform that gives artists and music companies a range of sales and fan relationship tools. It didn't hurt that high-profile acts like Arcade Fire, Barenaked Ladies, David Byrne, Brian Eno, Lenny Kravitz, and OK Go used the service.

Among other things, the Topspin service provides a shopping cart that can sell digital media, tickets, CDs, apparel, and other merchandise. It also allows artists to create embeddable widgets and custom audio/video streaming players linked to artist offers.

The site explains, "Topspin combines media management, fan management, distribution, sales reporting, and analytics in one environment."

31) Nimbit

www.nimbit.com

Anyone who says there are no music sales opportunities these days is delusional. Nimbit is yet another tool for music sales and fan engagement – and it's actually been around for a while. This service gives you a sales storefront that can be used on Facebook, Myspace and other sites, catalog management and soundscan reporting, and tools for messaging and tracking your fans.

In addition, Nimbit provides credit card processing, warehousing and fulfillment of physical orders; a complete website called Instant Band Site; and digital distribution on iTunes, Amazon, Rhapsody, and other online retailers.

32) Accept payments from your own website

You already know your fans can order your CDs securely online when you get set up with CD Baby, Amazon, and some of the other sites listed here. But what if you want to take orders directly from your own site? Here are three alternate payment processing services to consider using:

PayPal.com
www.paypal.com

Checkout by Amazon
payments.amazon.com

2CheckOut
www.2checkout.com

Look over fees and policies carefully. Most charge a per-transaction fee plus a percentage of each sale. PayPal has the lowest fees and most flexible access to your money. But look them all over and see what works for you.

To sum up: Open your mind to the music sales possibilities all around you ... and you may soon find yourself with a lot of extra closet space.

Chapter 14

The Easiest Way to Make Money in the Music Business

Most likely, you've been performing regularly, attracting some new fans, selling a few CDs or music downloads, and generally having a good time making music. In many ways, you're already successful and deserve to feel good about your accomplishments.

But there's also a good chance you have a nagging sense that something is missing. More specifically, you wish more money was coming in for all your efforts. If that describes you, you're not alone. At times it seems the majority of people who pursue creative passions aren't making the big bucks.

Even though this is a common situation for musicians, that doesn't mean you should accept it as your permanent state of being. There are many ways to increase the flow of money into your life through music.

Here's the secret formula: The most successful artists develop "multiple streams of income." The idea here is that small streams of cash from several different sources can eventually build into a steady, flowing river of revenue.

Crank up the money volume

In Barbara Winter's insightful book, *Making a Living Without a Job*, she discusses "multiple profit centers." Winter writes: "Rather than thinking in terms of having a single source of income (as we are trained to do when we see our income tied to a job), the savvy entrepreneur thinks about developing several income sources. With planning and an openness to additional opportunities as they come along – you can create as many streams as you desire."

To illustrate the point, Winter mentions Richard Branson, the founder of Virgin Records, who reportedly oversees more than 150 different small enterprises. And Branson keeps inventing new projects all the time.

Reality: Don't think you have to run an international corporation to make this tactic work. If we simply look at the standard ways an artist can earn income, this multiple profit center approach becomes clear.

A musical act can potentially make money from:

1) Live performance fees

2) CD and merchandise sales at live shows (and each piece of merchandise is a separate profit center)

3) CD sales through distributors and retail stores

4) CD and merchandise sales from the artist's own website

5) CD sales on Amazon.com, CD Baby, and other Internet music outlets

6) Digital sales through iTunes and other music download sites

7) Song placement in films and television

8) Fees from licensing your songs, name and image

9) Mechanical royalties on CD sales

10) Performance royalties (via ASCAP, BMI and SESAC)

11) Royalties from online music streams (via SoundExchange)

And these are just some of the ways.

Bottom line: The key to making a decent living with music lies in making sure that the many streams available to you are producing. Expecting your income only from live shows or only from iTunes sales to bring in a sufficient amount is risky at best. It's a lot easier, for instance, to generate $500 a month each from five different (but related) sources than it is to pray that one source will reel in the whole $2,500.

These multiple streams of income aren't limited to activities that involve your songs or band. What other skills and opportunities do you possess that you could leverage into extra cash? Can't think of any? Try again. Believe me, everyone has the potential to generate additional revenue – if he or she only searches for possibilities.

Example: Let's say you have a basement full of recording gear that you've turned into a quality home studio. Perhaps you use it to record your own band or solo projects and are now ready to offer your services to earn extra cash.

Of course, the obvious thing to do is make your services available to record other bands and songwriters who are looking for good, affordable recordings of their music. And many people with home recording setups do just that. The only problem is, that's all they do ... accept to complain that not enough paying customers are booking time.

The trick is to look outside the normal, predictable methods. To demonstrate this philosophy, here are 11 random ideas on how a person with a home studio could create multiple profit centers:

1) Copyright registration service

It seems everyone is confused about how to register a copyright with the Library of Congress (in the U.S.). It's not really that difficult, of course, but many of your studio clients may pay you a fee to do it for them and save them the trouble.

2) Recording classes

Do you feel competent enough to effectively share your knowledge of the recording process with others? If so, offer basic recording classes in your studio.

3) CD duplication

People who use your recording services are prime candidates for CD duplication. Offer that additional service to your customers and reap the rewards.

4) Voice-overs and spoken word

Music is not the only way to make money with a home recording studio. You can also reach out to customers who need to record voice-overs for radio commercials and instructional multi-media projects, as well as poets and authors wanting to produce spoken-word recordings of their work.

5) Soundtrack library

Many savvy musicians make extra money recording instrumental tracks that are used in the background of films, TV shows, video games, computer-based training materials, and more.

6) Compilation CDs

Most of your music customers are going to want to promote their songs after they have a finished product. Once you have a list of satisfied clients, offer to release a compilation CD of the best acts. The bands pay you a fee per song to put it all together. As long as the total fees you collect are more than your costs, you come out ahead – while helping a lot of acts get the notoriety they crave.

7) Equipment rental

I know, you would never think of parting with your new, expensive gear – even for a few hours. But surely, you have some equipment in your arsenal that you'd be comfortable renting to someone. This way, he or she gets to use the component for a reasonable fee, and you end up with an extra income source.

8) Audio birthday cards

Offer a special service whereby paying customers come in and record a personal greeting to a loved one. You could promote it as being a much more appealing gift than a typical, boring greeting card.

9) Audio restoration

Are you good with digital audio editing software? If so, find customers who need to restore old vinyl albums or want to convert scratchy analog audio programs to digital versions.

10) Mastering

Recording and mixing individual songs is just one part of the process. Before a full CD is replicated, all of the tracks need to be mastered so the whole collection has a cohesive, high-quality sound. Teach your customers the importance of mastering and offer that as an added source of income.

11) Morning radio show jingles and song parodies

I know this one can work because I've done it. Several years ago there was a local morning show team that paid me $100 to $200 a month to write and record song parodies and goofy jingles for them. It wasn't a huge amount of money, but it helped fill some financial gaps – and it was quite fun!

No matter where your special niche in the music business lies, there are literally dozens of related ways to earn extra cash. In her *Making a Living Without a Job* book, Barbara Winter suggests not trying to launch all of your new money-making ideas at one time. Pick the one you're most passionate about and get it going first. Once it's up and running, begin another profit center. Then another. Before long, you'll have a good number of these revenue centers working for you.

Note: Over time, however, you'll find some of your activities losing steam (or yourself losing interest) and it'll be time to drop them. That's why it's a good idea to always be thinking of new income-producing concepts.

In his book, *No More Cold Calls*, marketing expert Jeffrey Lant describes building what he calls the "mobile mini-conglomerate" – another phrase for this multi-pronged way of earning a living.

He suggests some of the following tactics for regularly developing new money-making opportunities:

- **Keep an idea file.** Whether it's in a notebook, file folder, shoebox or on your computer, have one designated place where you store all of your ideas for making extra money. This will pay big dividends and ensure that you don't lose or forget your best ideas.

- **Start an expert file.** Whenever you meet someone who may be able to help you in the pursuit of a money-making venture, make sure to ask for his or her name and contact info. This especially goes for people and companies with whom you might be able to work out lucrative cross-promotions.

- **Collect articles, books and publications about money.** In addition to music-related publications, make sure and expose yourself to a variety of titles on marketing and personal finance. As you read about success stories in other industries, always ask yourself, "How can this good idea be applied to my interests and skills in the music business?"

- **Get a brainstorming partner.** While you want to train your mind to be on the lookout for new opportunities, working by yourself all the time has its limitations. That's where having a brainstorming partner or two comes in handy. Ask your most creative and open-minded associates to join you in a think session, in which the main topic is coming up with new money-making ideas. You may be pleasantly surprised with the workable concepts that pop up during these meetings.

- **Keep records of what did and didn't work.** Creating another income steam can be exciting and challenging. But if the new profit center isn't producing, you'll just be spending your limited time and energy in vain. Keep a log of your start-up expenses, specific actions taken, and the bottom-line results of your efforts. Use this information to determine whether the new income stream is worth continuing.

If you're completely satisfied with your current income level, congratulations. You're in a select group. But if there's any discontent regarding your finances, the multiple-streams approach may be the best answer to help you overcome a cash-flow deficiency.

Chapter 15

25 Ways to Finance Your Next Recording Project, Music Video or Major Equipment Purchase

You've heard the expression "It takes money to make money." And sometimes it does. You've also heard horror stories about the complications of bank loans, business plans, lawyers, and meddling investors. And it's those negative mental associations that keep many aspiring music people from ever taking a stab at a big project – whether it's committing to an album release, buying a new sound and lighting system, producing a music video, or starting a small record label.

I can hear you now: "Man, I'm never going to be able to get a bank loan. And I wouldn't trust a power-hungry investor with my career. Why bother?" Well, I say don't let those perceived obstacles stop you from getting what you want!

For now let's forget about bank loans and high finance – although we will touch on them briefly in this chapter. Instead, let's think about more creative, street-level methods of raising money. Let's call it Guerrilla Music Financing, because we're going to be attacking this money-raising business from the ground level, where we can get a lot more accomplished by relying on our creativity.

Important note: The first thing to note about Guerrilla Music Financing is that – unlike the traditional road to investment capital, where a large lump sum of money comes from one almighty source – we guerrillas have to think in terms of combining a number of smaller money-raising streams into one sizable river of cash.

What follows is a list of 25 specific actions you can take to get money flowing toward your musical project.

Six ways to raise thousands of dollars yourself

This next statement might seem obvious, but it's an important one to grasp: The best source for funding your musical projects is *you*. By taking control of your own financing, you avoid having to answer to a co-signer or investor. The feeling of freedom alone will lighten the load of small sacrifices you may have to make along the way.

Here are six great ways to turn to yourself for money matters:

- ## Set aside a percentage of your day job salary

First, set up a special savings account at a bank for the exclusive purpose of building a Guerrilla Music Project Fund. Setting aside just $25 a week will give you about $650 in only six months. And while your money is growing and earning interest at the bank, you can use this time to scout around for the best possible deal on studio time, video production, sound systems, or whatever it is you want to invest in.

- ## Earn extra cash to stash for your project

Humans have an uncanny ability to get things done when they are truly motivated. Don't limit yourself by thinking within the confines of your present financial situation. Could you possibly earn extra money by giving guitar lessons, working as a studio session player, or gigging as a solo act?

There are dozens of ways for people in the music business to make extra cash with their talents. Don't be a victim of tunnel vision. Playing a paid gig is just one of many ways to profit from music. Do you have skills at home recording, publicity, website design, or even running sound and lights for other bands? Use your creativity. (See the previous chapter for more on this topic.)

Note: Earning an additional $25 a week would give you another $650 in six months – a total of $1,300.

- ## Sell your old equipment

Most musicians have at least some seldom-used equipment sitting around in the basement or garage. Some have quite a bit. Is there a good reason why you continue to hang on to it? If not, you may be cheating yourself out of the extra cash you could earn by selling it.

Run a classified ad, post notices at music stores in your area, or sell to the highest bidder on eBay or Craigslist. Blow the dust off of those old suckers, sell them, and add some money to your Guerrilla Music Project Fund.

Another possibility: Many record stores pay cash for decent pre-owned releases. And don't forget books, appliances, and other items you can part with. Use your head and cash in on stuff you already have!

- ## Spend less on gear – buy only what you need

The main point here is to be realistic. Just as you define your musical and creative needs, you should also assess your technical and production needs. Separate what you would like to have from what you actually need.

Key questions: Do you really require that 24-channel board when a 16-channel mixer would do the job for a lot less money? Is that $700 guitar effects rack something you really need? Or is advertising your new release in a national magazine really necessary, when you may be better off promoting it on a regional level, where it will have more impact and cost less?

- ## Get a bank loan or line of credit

If you have a good credit rating, you have the option of getting a bank loan. True, this is what you want to avoid if you truly embrace the "guerrilla" philosophy. But some musicians are more financially secure than others. If you have some monetary stability and are confident about your future in music – at least for the next couple of years – this is a tempting option. Just make sure you don't strap yourself with loan payments if the band breaks up or album sales aren't as brisk as you hoped.

Note: There are plenty of juicy guerrilla suggestions still to come in this chapter, and many of them will be even better, less-costly ways to get the funds you want.

- ## Use credit cards

Another method of financing is using a credit card. This is basically a loan, but I list it separately because many people overlook it as a financing option. You can either purchase items directly by charging them to the card or get a lump sum cash advance to spend on a variety of things.

Credit cards carry the same disadvantages of a loan, only those low minimum payments make the dangers of snowballing interest even greater. However, life is often a gamble and a lot of musicians have used credit cards to fund everything from PA and lighting purchases to entire album releases.

Example: I'll never forget the time I received a promotional mailing from a new artist. The flier read, "Sponsored by Visa, MasterCard and American Express" – pointing out, in a humorous way, that he was an independent artist funding his music project with his personal credit cards. It certainly caught my eye, and it definitely helped him get his music out into the world. So keep credit cards in mind, but use them cautiously.

Two more ways to raise money fast

- ## Solicit family members and friends

If you still need more funds after putting to use all the possibilities of raising cash yourself, the next safest bets are family members and friends. While borrowing money from relatives and acquaintances is a natural for some people, it can be a stomach-churning curse for others. So move slowly in this area.

Even though these casual investors are fronting you money because they care for and believe in you, you'd be wise to spell out everything on paper before accepting any friendly funding. Get it all in writing. Will you have to pay it back, and if so, when? How much input will Aunt Gertrude want on your next album if she's footing the bill? Find out ahead of time and you'll keep everyone happy.

• Seek out investors

Now we move into a more complicated realm. To attract investors, you usually have to come up with a written business plan that includes budgets, expenses, projected revenues, and countless other tedious details. If you're uncomfortable with numbers, fine print and selling yourself, traditional investment strategies might not work for you.

Most musical acts that attract investors basically end up making fans of people who have extra money to play with. In other words, investors should ideally have their hearts into what your music and vibe are all about.

Question: How do you find supportive investors? By being sociable and meeting all of your fans. It's that simple. Plus, don't be shy about mentioning to people that you're looking for an investor (or two, or five). In fact, many artists have found it's easier to find 10 people who each invest $1,000 than it is to search for one person who can invest the whole $10,000.

When you find interested parties, you must demonstrate that you and your music have merit and potential to make money for both you and the investor. Along with a business plan that spells out everything about your music career, clip articles from respected magazines on similar success stories and highlight industry trends based on information from trade publications. Also, it doesn't hurt to list a respected person in the music industry as your personal consultant.

Key: Agree ahead of time on what role the investor will play in your career. Will he or she be hands-on or more of a silent partner? Will the investor be reimbursed through an ongoing percentage of your earnings or only at a specific time, such as when you sell 2,000 CDs or downloads? Make sure the details are clear and beneficial to both parties, and have an attorney look over the final agreement.

Four more ways to get the financing you need

• Use your personal credit

Okay, so you don't have the financial clout to get a mega-bucks bank loan. Does that mean you're completely out of luck when it comes to getting credit? Maybe not.

Is there a music store, recording studio, or video producer in town who you've developed a good relationship with? If so, don't overlook the good possibility of getting personal credit from the owner of one of these establishments. This arrangement is basically an informal loan. The business owner, in essence, would give you the equipment, studio time, or service now ... with the understanding that you will pay the fee at a future date when you're able. As always, be specific on the repayment timetable and dollar amounts.

• Offer sponsorships

Coke, Pepsi, Miller Genuine Draft, and Bud Light aren't the only brand names that can sponsor musical events. Even though the corporate big guys are best known for it, why couldn't your local music store or studio sponsor you? You put up posters and pass out fliers promoting their businesses at your shows ... and they give you a discount or free stuff in exchange. What a concept!

• Practice the ancient art of barter

Do you have a skill, product or service that would be of value to a recording studio owner, video producer, newspaper publisher, or CD replicater? Well, if they have something you want, and you have something they want, it may be time to put the ancient art of trading goods and services into action. That's what bartering is all about, and it works perfectly for Guerrilla Music Financing. In fact, it may be one of your most powerful tactics for financing your music venture on a limited budget.

Another angle: What if the business owner isn't interested in what you can offer? You're next option would be what I call a Trade Triangle. Ask the owner what he'd be willing to barter for if there were no limits. Let's say a studio owner needs a new transmission on his car. Perhaps you know (or can find) a mechanic who might be interested in what you have to offer – maybe your band could play free at the company's upcoming anniversary street party.

Then you create a Trade Triangle. The mechanic gets free entertainment from you, the studio guy gets a new transmission, and you get your free recording time from the studio. Everybody's happy ... and without spending a dime! That's Guerrilla Music Financing at its best.

Three great ways to create cash if you're in a working band

• Save money from paying jobs

One of the best ways for a working band to raise a lot of cash for a major project is through paying gigs. Even a band that works part-time could easily come up with at least $500 a month from live shows – that's another $3,000 for your Guerrilla Music Project Fund in six months.

This method is a lot easier to manage, though, if the members don't depend on band job money for basic living expenses. If the members really need the steady cash, try setting aside a percentage of gig money from each job, even if it's only 10 to 20 percent. Just take it off the top before everyone gets paid.

• Promote fund-raising gigs

Non-profit companies, environmental coalitions, and charities of all types use fund-raising events to come up with the operating cash for their organizations. People generally like to do something constructive for a good cause, so they show up and donate money. Well, if this technique works for charities, it can also work for your musical act's fund-raising needs.

Strategy: Pick a night when you're booked at a local club or hall and promote it as a "Show Your Support Night." Ask your fans to play a part in your success story by helping you fund your next recording project. Have a suggested $20 donation at the door. Let attendees know that all the proceeds collected that night go toward financing the recording. Maybe even offer to list everyone's name in the album credits if they contribute.

You could also use this event to pre-sell your CDs – in effect, earning revenue before you've even produced them. Remember, you won't get things in life unless you ask for them. Just make sure to give something of value back in return.

• Launch a 30-day, fan-funding campaign online

One of the newest ways that artists are finding success raising money for creative projects is a trend called "crowd funding" or "fan funding." In essence, it involves taking the fund-raising event concept and moving it into the online realm. Only instead of a one-night event, artists can raise money directly from fans over a 30- or 60-day period (although evidence suggests that 30-day campaigns are most effective).

Elements of a successful campaign often include a welcome video explaining details of the project, along with a list of perks that people get when they commit funds at various price points. The higher the dollar amount a fan is willing to donate, the greater the perks (which can include free downloads, autographed CDs, private Skype performances, live house concerts, and more).

Many web-based services have sprouted up to serve this growing trend. As of this writing, Kickstarter is the most prominent site in the category. Here's a list of five such sites to consider:

Kickstarter
www.kickstarter.com

Indiegogo
www.indiegogo.com

Sellaband
www.sellaband.com

RocketHub
www.rockethub.com

PledgeMusic
www.pledgemusic.com

• Sell CDs, downloads, T-Shirts and merchandise

Your live shows can bring in a lot more money than just your performance fee or what you collect at the door in cover charges. If you and your act aren't taking full advantage of merchandising, you're missing the financial boat. Bands with even modest followings are reaping lots of extra money by selling T-shirts, caps, buttons, stickers, and more.

Obviously, if you're trying to raise money for a big recording project, you may not have a CD to sell yet. But if you do, by all means, push them doggies at your live shows. Mentioning them often and enthusiastically from the stage is a good start. But if you really want to cash in on merchandising, set up a booth or table chock full of everything you have to sell and make sure a friend, roadie or associate mans it the entire night.

Important note: If you're seriously using fund-raising and merchandising as a means to finance your next musical project, you'd be wise to take all the money earned through these methods and put it directly into your Guerrilla Music Project Fund account. And don't touch it until you're ready to invest in your specific project.

So you think this idea of raising cash from gig money and merchandising is great. But wait! What if your goal is to purchase a PA and light show? Without them, you can't play out to earn money. And without that extra money, you'll never be able to afford them. It's the ultimate Catch 22, right? *Wrong!* Here are some solid ways to play out and make money without your own system.

(*Note:* I admit, these next three suggestions are elementary, but I include them just in case you're overlooking them.)

• Work at clubs that have house systems

Many venues have their own in-house sound and lighting systems. By providing them, club owners can get bands to play for lower rates, since the band doesn't have to haul in and set up its own system. Your job, then, is to find the clubs in your area with house systems and try to get work in those venues first. By doing so, you'll get those paid jobs and merchandising opportunities – without needing your own PA and lights.

- ## **Work with bands that have systems**

While you're looking at venues with house systems, don't overlook other opportunities for paid work at other clubs. One way is to work with other bands that already have good sound and lighting systems. Whether you're opening, doing a split bill or headlining, try to align yourself with groups that will allow you to use their systems at shared gigs.

You may have to help cover the cost of the sound person or even do a little roadie work yourself. But that's a small price to pay, considering the other band is bringing in what you don't have. By using this arrangement, you'll open up your money-making possibilities to include practically any venue in your region.

- ## **Rent from stores, bands or discount services**

This may be another selection from the Overly Obvious category, but here it is anyway: When you have a paid gig beckoning and you don't have a sound or lighting system of your own, renting one or hiring someone to bring one in might be your best solution – especially if you know you'll earn more than you'll spend on the show.

Your options include renting PA and lights from music stores, sound companies or other bands and running them yourself. But don't forget about hiring a freelancer to come in and do all the dirty work for you ... at a higher price, of course. Some of the best deals may come from other bands that rent systems on their nights off (in fact, they may be doing it to build their own Guerrilla Music Project Funds).

Adding it all up

Let's figure out what a four-piece band might be able to raise in six months using just some of the techniques listed here. First, let's start with your potential as an individual. Suppose you were able to set aside just $20 a week from your day job for your Guerrilla Music Project Fund. You'd have just over $500 in six months. Then suppose you could earn an additional $20 a week giving lessons, doing home recording, or any number of things discussed earlier. That would give you another $500.

If you really tried, you could probably raise about $250 selling off some old equipment. And by trimming back some of your more extravagant musical buying habits, you should be able to redirect another $250 into the account over the six-month period. That gives you a total of $1,500 in six months using only your own discipline and ingenuity.

Do the math: Even though you could easily raise still more money by getting a credit card cash advance or a $500 to $1,000 loan from a family member, let's use the more conservative $1,500 individual figure for our purposes. Now multiply that number by the four people in our four-member example band. Suddenly we've got $6,000 in the collective Guerrilla Music Project Fund.

And we haven't even factored in fund-raising gigs, paid band jobs, and merchandise sales. Over the course of six months, a band could easily raise another $3,000 from these sources. Add that to the previous subtotal and you'd be on your way to raising nearly $10,000 for your next project!

10 ways to get a better price on equipment

You've heard the saying: A penny saved is a penny earned. It's true. Don't spend more than you have to on equipment. Use these tips and save.

- ## Buy used gear

Finding good, pre-owned equipment can suit your needs and be a lot easier on your pocketbook at the same time. Shop around and test the stuff before you buy. Also check out Craigslist at www.craigslist.org.

- ## Shop by mail order

Ordering gear by mail can often get you lower prices while allowing you to avoid paying in-state sales tax. Here are three good mail order equipment sources:

Musician's Friend
www.musiciansfriend.com
(800) 449-9128

zZounds
www.zzounds.com
(800) 996-8637

eBay – Musical Instruments
http://instruments.shop.ebay.com/

- ## Pay cash up front

No secret here. If you've done a good job of setting aside money for your Guerrilla Music Project Fund, walking into a store or studio with cash in hand will always give you plenty of leverage to get a great, low price.

- ## Compare prices and shop around

I don't mean to insult your intelligence here, but too often many of us get hooked on the first offer we come across ... and quite often it's not the best buy. Resist impulse buying and check out other options before you commit.

- ## Establish a relationship with one retailer or studio

On the other end of the spectrum from shopping around is being loyal to one business ... that is, if it rewards you for your patronage with lower prices. If you've done a noticeable amount of business with one particular music dealer in town, ask about a preferred customer discount.

- **Consider display models**

Ranking right up there with used equipment bargains is the super price you can often get on demo models. Eventually, stores have to dispose of the display units that sit on the sales floor. And they move them by letting somebody walk out with these items at a 30- to 70-percent discount. That somebody might as well be you!

- **Take advantage of sales, liquidations and going-out-of-business specials**

Keeping an ear to your regional music grapevine might help alert you when a retailer is going out of business. When this occurs, you can bet the business owner will be more than eager to sell remaining equipment at deep discounts.

- **Buy at wholesale by helping a store meet its quota**

When music stores buy equipment from suppliers, the discount they get depends on the total amount of gear the store purchases. The higher the dollar amount, the better the wholesale price. Knowing this, why not offer to buy that monster PA system from the store at wholesale cost, which might help the store up its purchasing power and get a bigger discount from its supplier? It's worth a shot.

- **Work at a music store**

Sure, why not? As an employee, you'll probably get a discount on any purchases you make while you work for the store. Plus you'll get a paycheck from the store! Yet another option.

- **Haggle ... and ask for a better price!**

This one was added because too many people simply forget to do it. The number listed on the price tag is, more often than not, negotiable. And if you never ask for a lower price, it certainly won't be offered to you. So ask ... and you just might receive a great price break.

Congratulations!

You've made it through all 25 creative ways to finance your next music project. What you need to do now is go through the couple dozen money-making and money-saving suggestions in this chapter (by the way, feel free to add some of your own) and start deciding which methods are going to work best for you.

Some musicians have access to investors while others feel stronger about going the merchandising route. Some are in a better position to set aside cash from their day jobs while others opt for a credit card advance.

Key principle: Remember the river of Guerrilla Music Financing we covered at the beginning of this chapter? The best money-raising plan will incorporate several different streams. A little savings here, some extra revenue there ... it all adds up.

Your new action plan

Finally, I'd like to talk about one of the most important aspects of raising money in the music business: setting weekly and monthly goals. Once you narrow down your financial plan of attack, put it on paper. Give yourself a specific amount of money you want to raise and a date by which you want to have the total in your Guerrilla Music Project Fund.

Then make sure and open a separate bank account for this special fund. I suggest using at least a six-month plan and being realistic about the dollar amounts. Setting unattainable goals will do nothing but wear down your confidence in reaching them.

Next, break up the dollar amounts into monthly and weekly figures. In other words, calculate how much you're going to have to earn or set aside each week in specific categories to hit your target amount. Breaking it up into bite-size chunks makes any worthy goal more manageable and keeps you on track week after week in your pursuit of it.

Other considerations: When it comes to sponsorships, bartering and other less-tangible methods, write out your specific action plan: who you'll contact, when you'll reach out to them, what offer you'll make, etc. Once these steps are taken and a response is received, it's time to reevaluate the plan. Just as an airplane pilot readjusts his flight pattern many times before reaching a specific destination, so should you adjust your financial action plan along the way to reaching your money goals.

Where will you go from here?

The choice is now yours. If you don't consider all the money-raising possibilities and write out a plan to begin with, you'll continue to stray (like so many people) down a wandering path to musical obscurity. Not creating your personal road map and being committed to it week after week, month after month, will lead you to *not* getting that new release out, *not* getting that music video produced, or *not* getting that killer sound system you need.

But since you now have more than two dozen solid ideas at your fingertips, along with a newfound commitment to reach your financial and creative goals, you'll be one of the smart ones basking in the glow of having attained yet another one of your musical dreams.

Chapter 16

How to Double Your Music Sales (in 90 Days or Less)

If you've gone through the trouble of recording your music and making it available for sale, you no doubt want to sell some of it. Preferably, a lot of it. Question: Would you be better off if you could double the amount of music you currently sell? Of course, you would. This chapter is filled with a couple dozen ways to make that happen over the next 90 days or less.

Disclaimer: You may notice that many of the steps outlined here are echoed in other chapters as well. But that's okay. They are important points that warrant repeating.

Write great songs and create meaningful music

While the purpose of this chapter does not include songwriting advice, it should be noted that all the marketing help in the world won't be effective unless the music you make profoundly touches people. Writing great music that connects with your target audience needs to be one of your driving forces. So make sure you spend plenty of time and creative energy on this crucial area.

Put a priority on planning and execution

Think of these twin soldiers as your offensive line. Planning (knowing where you want to go and what route you'll take to get there) and execution (marching toward your goal by taking decisive action) are the key ingredients you'll need to double your music sales. Set weekly and monthly sales goals, and monitor your progress regularly to make sure you're on track.

Bring back past customers

It costs about six times the money and effort to win over a new fan as it does to stay connected to someone who has bought your music in the past or been to one of your shows. Don't overlook this gold mine. Keep in touch with and send special offers to people who have previously spent money on you. They are, by far, the most likely group of people to spend money on you again today.

Upsell current customers

Okay, so someone comes to a gig, buys your latest album, and signs up on your mailing list. Now what? Time to move on to the next new customer, right? Wrong.

Send your current buyers a special offer to also get your previous releases and merchandise.

Insight: Your first or second album may be old news to you, but it will probably be fresh and enjoyable to a new fan. He or she likes your music and even bought your latest CD or download. Don't deny them the pleasure of getting even more of your music – both old and new. Strike while the music sales iron is hot. It's called "upselling," and you'll have to start doing it if you really want to double your music sales.

Always cultivate new customers

Music marketing is a juggling act. You have to simultaneously be courting past fans and nudging current buyers while always being on the lookout for new fans to bring into the fold. You cultivate these new people by:

- Encouraging mailing list sign-ups at gigs

- Talking to the people who attend your live shows

- Constantly soliciting fan email newsletter subscriptions online

- Giving solid reasons for editors, writers and reviewers to cover you

- Swapping website links and email newsletter blurbs with other related websites and artists

- Putting your contact info on every promotional item you distribute

- Generally making it easy for people to find you and get in touch

In short, make a commitment to being a fan-building machine.

Identify your most profitable selling areas

In order to double your music sales in 90 days, you must know where and how to concentrate your energies. First, consider if geography will play a part. Will you most likely sell more music locally? In warmer climates? Along the East Coast? In Denmark? Next, consider the method of sales: at live shows, on the Internet, through retail outlets ... which ones will work best for you?

Understand who your ideal fans are

Determine what type of person is most likely to spend money on you: young or old, men or women, lavish tastes or budget-minded, hyper or mellow? Other questions to ask: Do these people have the money to buy your music? And is this segment of the population growing in number or shrinking? Are there any other ways of positioning your music to also appeal to a different group of people? Write down answers to these questions, brainstorm, and zero in on fans who have the interest and money to buy your music.

List ways of getting access to your fans

Once you know exactly what type of music fan you're going after, make a list of various ways to communicate with these specific people. What magazines and newspapers do they read? Where do they hang out? What radio stations do they listen to? What retail outlets do they frequent? What websites do they visit? What blogs and podcasts do they subscribe to?

List every conceivable way of reaching these important folks. Then design an action plan to make the most of these avenues.

Tour and play live often

Sure, this is a no-brainer, but are you making the most of every possibility? First, are you playing out a lot locally and regionally? Does your touring plan make sense? The best approach is to either spiral out slowly from your home base, or target specific cities you will play on a regular schedule. The more areas you're known in, the better your chances of selling more music.

Other options: What about unplugged shows at record stores, coffeehouses, and more offbeat locations like bookstores and art galleries? Refer back to the list of places where your fans hang out and try to perform at those venues.

Make the most of retail store tie-ins

Have you visited all of the important music shops and arranged to have your CDs sold there? If so, do managers have sample copies for in-store play? If the store has a listening station, can you get your disc featured on it? Will the store use discount coupons for your release as a bag stuffer (maybe in exchange for you distributing coupons for the store at your gigs)? Be creative and sell more music!

Pursue radio exposure of any kind

Of course, you can mail unsolicited CDs and hound program directors until they either play your songs or you give up trying. Or you can use some often-overlooked tactics to get on the air: Supply stations with several of your CDs to give away as part of an on-air promotion. Write and record a humorous theme song for high-profile shows and on-air personalities.

Find a current event tie-in to one of your songs and get interviewed on the air about it. Ask nightclub owners who advertise to use your songs in the background of their radio and TV commercials. Buy cheap overnight ads to promote your new release. Sponsor a targeted podcast or community radio show.

Promote inexpensive sampler CDs

Put together short, inexpensive sampler CDs of your best songs and either give them away to potential fans (in exchange for a name and email address) or sell them for a buck or two at live shows. You may not make money on this tactic upfront, but if you follow up and persuade even 5 to 10 percent of the people who take home your sampler to buy your full-length album, it could be well worth it.

Better idea: Team up with four other artists and produce a compilation sampler CD. You'll benefit from the combined promotional efforts of all five acts.

Squeeze all you can out of the Internet

The Web has most definitely become the great equalizer. No secret here. It's easier than ever for independent artists to reach a worldwide audience. A big chunk of online activity is dedicated to music, and it seems there are more sites every month that sell indie music or cater in some way to unsigned acts. You need to be using the Internet to spread the word about your music. Thousands of artists are already doing it. Now go get your share!

Here are some steps you can take to sell more of your music online:

Get your own domain name

While there are many music websites that will offer you a free page or section, your best bet is to register your own domain name and direct it to wherever you choose to host your pages. There are two big benefits:

- A web address like www.JohnSmithMusic.com carries more credibility and is easier to remember than a long and winding address like www.musichotspot.com/music/johnsmith.

- Websites that offer free music profiles don't owe you anything. If you suddenly find your page is missing, you usually have no recourse. It's fine to set up profiles on these sites, just don't use any of them as your primary home on the Web.

Registered domains are simply taken more seriously. And rates have never been cheaper. One of the most popular sites for registering low-cost domain names is **Go Daddy** (www.godaddy.com). Fees are only about $10 USD per year. **DirectNIC** (www.directnic.com) is another good one, with domain name fees around $15 a year.

Publish a fan email newsletter

Websites and other digital destinations are great, but you have to rely on fans to remember and visit often. That's a very passive form of marketing. To sell more music, you absolutely must collect the names and email addresses of people who have willingly agreed to get regular follow-up messages on your musical activities.

Therefore, you have to promote your free music newsletter consistently. Offer people incentives to sign up. Having a large and growing subscriber list is one of your biggest keys to online sales and notoriety.

To help manage your list, here are some services to consider:

HostBaby
www.hostbaby.com

Bandzoogle
www.bandzoogle.com

ReverbNation
www.reverbnation.com

FanBridge
www.fanbridge.com

TinyLetter
www.tinyletter.com

MailChimp
www.mailchimp.com

Make sure your music is available in all the major online e-tailers

Every now and then I run across a musician who has a misguided idea. He or she says, "iTunes and Amazon take such a big cut, I'm going to sell my music only from my own website, where I get to keep a lot more of the money."

This is a big mistake, unless you already have a huge, loyal fan base that would be willing to unquestionably buy directly from you. But if you're reading this book, there's a good chance you're not quite there yet. Allow fans to buy your music in the way that's most comfortable and familiar to them. That means you should make your music available for sale on all the popular music destinations, especially iTunes and Amazon.

And it's never been easier to do. For digital distribution to iTunes and many other online music stores, my favorite option is CD Baby at www.cdbaby.com. To get music on Amazon.com, consider either www.createspace.com or www.amazon.com/advantage.

And, for a great way to sell music directly from your site, check out **Bandcamp** at www.bandcamp.com.

See Chapter 13 for more details on these and other ways to sell more music.

Make free digital samples of your music available

Despite what you think of legal battles over the widespread sharing of digital music files, to sell more music online you have to make at least some of your music readily available ... for free. Getting fresh ears to experience your music is a challenge. Don't put up obstacles by hoarding it all to yourself.

But you don't have to give away the whole store. Make at least three songs from your album available in an MP3 format. After fans hear your digital music samples, direct them to where they can buy your entire album.

To summarize, if you want to sell more of your music online, you should:

1) Put up an artist website with a music sales page, show schedule, photos, and more.

2) Encourage fans to sign up for your free email newsletter – then send monthly updates that are filled with your personality and compelling sales offers.

3) Have clear links to your MP3 audio files and streaming players so people can hear your sounds immediately.

4) Make sure your music is available for sale at the most popular online destinations.

Find a healthy balance between selling and sharing

When your goal is to double your music sales, you have to step up and be more proactive in letting people know what you have for sale. And you have to create incentives for people to get off the fence and make a purchase. But you can take this concept too far and inadvertently alienate many of your fans.

What you want to avoid is thinking that marketing consists of bombarding people with a series of announcements: "We're playing at Joe's Bar this Friday night!" ... "New album on sale now!" ... "Click here to buy the T-shirt!"

Yes, a big part of making money with music is asking for the sale. But if that's all you do, you won't build trust and a likeability factor with your fan base. Don't think that you have to always "sell" to your fans. Instead, your main goal should be to "share" yourself with your fans. Share your music, your personal life, and insights into your musical journey. Ask fans questions and engage with them in a personal way.

When you mix in sales messages with a primarily personal approach, you'll find your music sales will increase.

Make appealing offers to fans to buy your music now

When you do send a sales message to your fan email list, go beyond just saying, "Hey, we have a new album. If you want it, click the Buy Now button." True, that is being proactive and you are asking for the sale. The fan can buy it now or next week or next year. They'll get around to it when they can.

Here's a better way: Make a special offer that creates a good reason for them to buy now instead of later: "Order by November 10 and get FREE shipping" or "The first 25 orders get autographed copies." Use the age-old influence of scarcity. Every so often, send an offer based on a limited time or a limited quantity. You may be surprised by how many more people order your music when you try this.

Create incentives for your fans to buy more

Inspiring fans to buy your music now will definitely move you toward doubling your music sales in 90 days. If you want to crank things up even more, also give a good reason to spend more money while they're in a buying frame of mind.

Here are some offers that will accomplish this: "For $10 extra, we'll also throw in our newest T-shirt (a $25 value)" or "Buy one CD, get a second copy at half off to give to a friend" or "Get all five of our albums and save 50%."

Getting fans to buy now is great. Inspiring them to spend a little more when they do is even better.

Use testimonials and positive quotes

Whether you're sending a sales message to fans or a plea to the media to cover you, don't depend on your own words alone to make your point. Use quotes from satisfied fans, positive reviews, or favorable comments from respected industry pros to back up your claims of worthiness. If more artists did this, they'd make more of an impression and sell a lot more music.

Determine your sales goal and display it

If you don't choose a specific sales goal and make a commitment to it, chances are your money-making progress will stall. To avoid this, write down your new action plan to double your music sales and post it prominently on the wall of your office or rehearsal area. Look at this plan every day and affirm your dedication to achieving it.

Set a target number of units

To hit a target, you must be able to see the bull's-eye clearly. To reach your music sales goals, you must have a number to aim for. First, determine your current level of sales. Let's say you now sell an average of 200 CDs and 300 single downloads a month.

In order to double your sales figures, you'd have to sell 400 CDs and 600 downloads a month. When you break it down, that amounts to about 93 CDs and 140 downloads a week. Knowing these hard facts will focus your energies and allow you to know exactly where you stand.

Check your progress and adjust the plan as needed

As you move through the next 90 days, measure your progress regularly. What's getting the best results? What's not working so well? How can you most effectively increase sales with a wise use of your current resources? What changes, if any, need to be made to reach the goal within 90 days?

You'll be able to keep track of music goals like this using the free Guerrilla Music Marketing worksheets that supplement this book. Just go to worksheets.thebuzzfactor.com to grab them.

Conclusion: Independent artists around the world are selling hundreds and thousands of CDs and downloads every month. There's no reason you shouldn't be among their ranks right now!

We covered a lot in these first four sections of the book. But we aren't finished yet. The fifth and final section reveals a final flurry of low-cost, creative guerrilla music promotion examples and strategies.

Section 5:
Guerrilla Music Promotion Tactics

Chapter 17

12 Low-Cost, High-Impact Music Promotion Ideas That Work

Recognition! Respect! A legion of loyal fans! Those are the rewards that most working musicians aspire to have. Yet, I've lost count of the number of frustrated artists I've encountered who work hard at their music but end up playing to empty rooms and accepting low income as a way of life.

Of course, you already know that any musical act must first have great songs, a defined musical identity, and an engaging live show to have half a chance at making a splash with fans and the media. Therefore, it's no surprise when bands that lack those elements don't cut it.

Question: But how many times have you seen (or been in) a killer band and said to yourself, "This group really deserves to have a crowd. People don't know what they're missing"? More than a few times, right?

The problem with these artists is that they miss the big picture and concentrate almost entirely on the music – which is admirable, but it leaves the marketing aspects of their music to chance. Long ago, I made a decision that I wanted more control over my career. I no longer depend on the whims of fate to steer my life. I suggest you embrace this same attitude.

Bottom line: Getting a grip on the promotional aspects of your music stacks the deck in your favor. Marketing helps you grab the attention of new fans and gets your music into their ears. Spending energy on creative promotional activities cranks your career into overdrive. When you market yourself effectively, you're able to spend more time making great music and less time rolling the dice and hoping a crowd shows up.

Another thing: Attention-getting tactics don't have to be complicated or expensive. You just have to think beyond simply pinning up fliers, slapping up a website, and letting some of your friends know about your gigs. Also, it's important to realize that no one promotional effort is going to work miracles. The low-budget, grass-roots music marketing approach that I advocate is a long-term, ongoing activity – not a one-shot deal.

Important note: Music marketing is a lot like multi-track recording. Each layer you create adds to the layers already put down. That's why you need to develop and deploy an ongoing series of promotional campaigns – with each one reaching more people and making them more familiar with your name, image and sound.

What follows is a list of 12 low-cost ideas you can use to promote your music, in addition to the many strategies you discovered earlier in the book. Hopefully, reading these methods will inspire you to use them and come up with even better marketing tactics of your own.

1) Hold a contest related to your band or release

Can you come up with a fresh idea to fire up the competitive spirit of music fans? The band Symon Asher did. This Seattle, WA-based group held a contest some years ago to guess the origin of its name. To register, people had to visit local record stores and fill out an entry form. Clues on the band's name were sent weekly to radio stations and the music press, creating even more of a buzz about the band.

Why it works: There are five effective angles to this promotional scheme:

- Forcing interested fans to register at record stores puts those contestants right smack in the middle of the music-buying environment, where they can easily listen to and buy your album.

- By bringing more people into their shops, record store owners have more incentive to promote the contest in-house, giving you even more exposure to music consumers.

- Since the contest is about nothing but the band's name, the publicity benefit is priceless: name recognition!

- By hanging onto all the entry forms, the band has a solid collection of fresh names to add to its mailing list.

- Getting the media involved by sending them clues to give to their audiences adds yet another layer of exposure – one that most publicists would die for.

This strategy could work just as well online, only you'd have fans register at your website. Find a way to make the contest idea work for you. It could just as easily be applied to the title of a song or new album too.

(By the way, if you're dying to know, the band mentioned above was named after the birth name of former Cream bassist/vocalist Jack Bruce, who was born John Symon Asher.)

2) Play the extremes: go really big or get really small

Most of the time, playing in the middle won't serve you well. You blend in or stay stuck in a homogenous pattern. Sometimes, playing the extremes can help you cut through and serve the needs of a different audience.

Let's consider what people use to watch television. In the middle are a lot of average-size TV screens. But on the edges you'll find extremes. On one end are the huge flat screen TVs and home theater systems. On the other are iPods and smart phones with tiny screens that play video. They all serve a need and appeal to certain people at different times.

Live musical offerings are no different. In the middle is the four-piece band. On the edges you'll find a range of choices – from solo acts and duos to big bands and symphony orchestras.

Great examples: CD Baby's DIY Musician blog once featured some Portland, OR, acts that exemplify this idea. One of them is Nick Jaina, a songwriter who has learned the value of being versatile. He plays out with a full band but also performs solo on the street for tips. Being able to get small pays off.

As Jaina states in the article, "That way, you can do your big rock show at the club AND do a simple acoustic set for the local radio station, for the cool indie record store, or for passersby on the street."

On the other extreme is MarchFourth, described as a "mobile big band spectacular." Along with a huge lineup that includes saxophones, trumpets, trombones, a drum/percussion corp, and more … the group is accompanied by stilt-walkers, dancing girls, flag twirlers, clowns, and acrobats.

"The onslaught of visual and audio sensations is stunning," reads the article, which goes on to deliver this gem:

The lesson here: Create something memorable! Do something dramatic. Do something at your show that people just aren't going to see [at] someone else's concert, something they won't get from the TV or Xbox, something that must be captured in the moment.

Consider what it is that only YOU do. Now magnify that thing so everyone in the crowd can feel it, whether you're a solo singer-songwriter or a traveling funk-rock circus.

Great advice. Don't play in the middle. Go to the edges. And get really small or go really big!

3) Teach your fans something

I know what you're thinking: "I'm an artist. I'm a performer. Why should I bother thinking about what I can teach my fans? My purpose is to entertain them."

True. That is your role. But an equally important activity is communicating with your fans in meaningful ways. When done right, that involves more than just promoting upcoming shows and letting people know where they can purchase your music.

Whether you know it or not, you have skills, talents, and first-hand knowledge of things that many people (especially your fans) would love to hear about and learn from. Why not start sharing some of your unique perspective in the form of how-to videos or blog posts?

Admittedly, this is not the first angle most music people think of when promoting themselves. But I encourage you to consider creating some of the following things:

• a video showing how to play your primary instrument (especially a specific popular song related to your style)

• a blog post on the history of your genre (or some little-known aspect of it)

• a video or blog post about how to best listen to and appreciate music in your specific genre

• a tutorial on the technique you used to record your song, video, or special effect

Examples:

Adrian Galysh is a Los Angeles-based guitarist. His video called "The Scale That Will Change Your Life" has been viewed more than 100,000 times. By teaching a technique that helped him greatly, he has connected with more aspiring guitarists … and more fans.

Amy Heidemann from the duo Karmin (featured in Chapter 8) is known for wearing a 1940's-inspired hair style called a "suicide roll." After being asked by many fans how she does it, Amy posted a tutorial video on YouTube showing exactly how. Nearly 2 million views later, it has proven to be a smart move.

So … What could you teach your fans that would truly engage them?

Yes, you're an artist and an entertainer. But you also have special information that your fans (and potential future fans) might love hearing about. So get comfortable with your new role as a teacher … and get ready to convert your students into hardcore fans!

4) Take advantage of free entertainment listings

Most cities in America have at least one newspaper that covers some aspect of local music and entertainment. And almost all of these publications offer free listings of who's playing where and when – commonly called the "entertainment calendar" section. Many cities also have websites dedicated to listing upcoming events. Believe it or not, live music calendar sections are well read. So why doesn't every artist take advantage of them?

Perhaps many musicians figure their fans will automatically do all the work necessary to seek them out. Maybe the band members are comfortable with their current level of popularity. Perhaps they think the venue will submit the dates to these websites and the media. (Ha! Guess again.) Maybe they are too busy and simply forget to submit their calendar information.

Key question: What good does it do to pour your heart and energy into practicing a mind-blowing set and then do very little to get people out to witness it? Take advantage of every free marketing opportunity available to you; they all contribute to your visibility. So find out how and where you can post your live show dates for each publication and website ... and then submit your schedule regularly!

5) Sponsor an award or special ceremony

Is there a distinguished person in your community you'd like to honor? Or is there an anniversary, special date in history, or cause you'd like to recognize? If so, plan a musical event around your chosen theme and make a party out of it.

Under normal circumstances, the local media couldn't care less about your regular weekend gig at Barney's Bar & Grill. But give them a one-time event with a news hook – such as a tribute, awards ceremony, etc. – and you just might get their attention.

6) Sponsor a college or community radio show

Public and community radio stations exist in most major cities these days. Like their PBS television cousins, one of their purposes is to expose segments of the culture that don't get covered in the mainstream media – and that includes local, independent music. These community stations air a wide variety of programs, many of which are sponsored by local businesses. Well, if a local business can sponsor a show, why couldn't an independent artist?

Sure, it will cost you some money, but it will probably be a lot less than advertising on a commercial station. And you'll be reaching a highly targeted audience – as long as you sponsor a show that attracts the types of people who make up your fan base.

7) Create innovative themes for your live shows

If your fans want to hear you play perfectly, they'll listen to your album. When they want a great live experience, they'll buy a ticket to your show.

But many musicians think the live experience is something that emanates only from the stage. However, an indie artist named Jennings knew better. She added a unique twist when she decided to combine a clothing swap with a recent performance in Nashville.

At first you may be a bit baffled. But she explains everything clearly on the Facebook event page she created to promote the show:

For those of you who don't know about clothing swaps, it's basically a great way to clean out your closet and pick up some used-but-new-to-you clothing.

Bring any unwanted clothing and save five dollars on your cover ($10 but $5 with old clothes) and you will be given a bag that allows you to take what you want! It's a sweet deal!

And all during the swap you will be able to hear some great music. Don't worry, if you don't want to take part in the swap, that's cool too! Just come and hang out for an evening of great music.

After seeing this "outside the clothes hamper" thinking, it really made me wonder. What other "theme night" concepts could you combine with your show to pack a unique entertainment value into each ticket sale?

Questions: Could you organize a food drive? A petting zoo? A mud-wrestling match? Or maybe a musical version of Eight-Minute Dating? A Heavy Metal Karaoke Smackdown? A Disco Trivia Night?

The further you push the boundaries, the more everyone will talk about it. So put on your thinking cap and get creative!

8) Record a seasonal or current events song

Unless you have friends in high places, your independent album barely stands a chance of getting radio airplay on commercial stations. Even the college and community stations require a lot of effort to get a substantial number of spins on the airwaves.

One way to sneak into a station's rotation is to use your creativity and come up with a novelty song that relates to a current topic in the news or an upcoming holiday. For instance, Christmas songs almost always get some airplay during the Yuletide season. But stretch further.

Optional approach: Since you may have a lot of competition during the Christmas season, try doing songs that pay tribute to more musically obscure holidays – such as Thanksgiving or Groundhog Day. (Come on, how many Groundhog Day songs can you think of?) And what about Easter, Presidents' Day or Columbus Day?

More ideas: What about songs pertaining to a local political scandal, sports team or election? How about putting a local slant on Halloween, the Fourth of July, or Valentine's Day? Or have you considered recording a jingle or theme song for one of the popular morning radio shows? Use your imagination. Anything is possible with this marketing angle.

Believe it or not, novelty songs have a much better chance of getting commercial airplay – which will get your name out there and possibly pave the way for your more serious songs later. Just make sure the novelty or theme song you write and pitch to the station is in line with your overall musical style and identity.

9) Use Skype or Ustream performances as a sales perk or fundraising incentive

Looking for something new and fresh to add to your next music sales offer to fans, or perhaps to use as an incentive for a fan-funding campaign? How about a live Skype or Ustream video performance?

Most live performance offers I see are literally live, in the flesh. For instance, with Kickstarter fundraising campaigns, many artists will offer to come play live at a donor's house at upper levels of support (like in the $500 to $5,000 range). And that often involves travel.

But what if you offered to do a personal performance for certain people via Skype or Ustream (or Apple's FaceTime or a Google+ Hangout)? You could offer more of them and at a lower price point – and never have to leave the house!

Also think outside of the fundraising campaign: Is this something you could offer to your more supportive fans at any time? For $100, you'll hook up live and sing someone a couple of special songs on his or her birthday (or some other special occasion).

Try it. You'll never know if there's a demand until you *ask your fans*!

10) Target specific cities and regions for best results

You don't need to do live shows across the country, coast to coast, to effectively tour and promote your music. In fact, it will probably be better for your exposure level and music sales (not to mention your sanity) to zero in on a predetermined number of cities.

Example: "You shouldn't spread yourself too thin," says Rob Squires, bassist for the Denver, CO-based Big Head Todd & the Monsters. Before landing its record deal years ago, the band took this approach: "To establish ourselves, we'd hit Chicago, San Francisco, Austin and the Colorado cities every other month," Squires told *Fast Forward*, a newsletter put out by Disc Makers.

Result: "Our plan worked out great. There'd be more and more people at shows each time we revisited those target cities." By focusing on a limited number of geographic areas, Big Head Todd & the Monsters was able to build a following and later signed with a record label that could give them nationwide support.

11) Ask venues to play your songs in their radio and TV commercials

Of all the venues at which you perform, at least some of them probably advertise on radio and television. And practically all of those commercials use music underneath an announcer's voice or video, right? Why not encourage the club owner to use one of your original songs for that purpose?

Lesson: It's the next best thing to being put into regular rotation on a radio station, even though you'll only be able to squeeze a verse and chorus, at most, into a commercial. But just think, you won't have to pull teeth with a program director and compete with hundreds of other new releases to get your music on the air. All you have to do is sell the idea to the venue owner.

Warning: You might have to negotiate with the owner to get this special treatment – remember, he or she is footing the bill for the paid ad spot. Some things to offer might include performing at the club for a reduced fee or offering part of your pay to help cover some of the ad costs. Either way, it might be worth it to get a minute of your original music on commercial radio or TV.

12) Ask your fans to help you get gigs and airplay

A wise person once said, "You won't get things in life unless you ask for them." Use that same philosophy when it comes to your fans. Don't be shy about asking the people who like your music the most to be a part of your success story.

There are two key ways to accomplish this:

- In all of your mailings to your fans, include the call letters and phone number of radio stations (or the web address and email for online shows and podcasts) you are targeting for airplay. Then encourage your fans to contact these stations and request that your music be played. You can also distribute fliers at your live shows that offer this same radio contact information.

- While you're asking your fans for help with airplay, why not ask for their help in getting paid gigs? You never know who among your fans knows a

155

venue owner or someone having a private function with a budget for live music. You might even entice your fans further by offering a 10 percent commission on whatever you make through the job they help you book. Why not? Try it and see what happens.

Action step: Take these 12 promotional ideas and make them work for you!

Chapter 18

How to Use the Telephone More Effectively to Get Paid Gigs, Radio Airplay, and Media Coverage

No doubt about it, the telephone is still one of the most powerful tools you can use to turbo-charge your music career. Even with modern communication alternatives like email, text messaging and video conferencing, the phone is still the workhorse of methods available to promote your music.

This leads to some good news and bad news concerning all this business of dialing for dollars (and exposure). First, the bad news: Virtually everyone has a telephone, which means that millions of people are already using the phone to compete with you in your quest to get media coverage, airplay, paying gigs, and music sales.

Now the good news: While all of these people are cluttering the phone lines with their messages, many of them are using weak (and even harmful) tactics with Mr. Bell's fine invention. This sets the stage for people who know the tricks and nuances of telephone marketing to get ahead by using it effectively.

I've lost track of the times I've received calls from poor, misdirected fools who open a conversation with, "Hello, is this Bob Barker?" My response: "No, he's the game show host, but I do encourage you to have your cats and dogs spayed and neutered." (Mr. Barker is an animal right proponent.)

Then there was the caller who once asked my office manager, "What issue of the *Riverfront Times* [a competing newspaper in town] will my album review run in?" Her response: "Why don't you call them to find out?"

Question: Can you see how this rampant and mindless abuse of the phone can work against so many people? And how easy it would be to stand out from the pack and get more of what you want by doing your homework and using a few simple telephone marketing tactics?

Start putting the following suggestions to use in your music promotion efforts and you won't have to worry about calling anyone a game show host again.

Go through a mini-rehearsal before the call

In the same way that your band sounds a lot less polished when you haven't been practicing, so will your telephone presentation be rusty if you haven't prepared beforehand.

Solution: Simply take a minute before each call and consider what your objective is and the approach you'll use. When calling on a nightclub owner, stumbling around with vague phrases such as "Um, hey, you don't know me but ... uh, I play in a band ... and I was wondering what it would take to get my band to play your club ..." won't get you any closer to that gig.

What will help is identifying your objective: trying to get an opening slot for a specific band, wanting to establish a relationship with the talent booker, persuading the owner to set aside a night to hold a benefit concert, etc. Also, plan what approach you'll take: mentioning mutual friends and the recommendations they've given, offering to drop by at a convenient time to meet for 10 minutes, having a list of bands who've agreed to play a benefit, and so on.

Choose one specific objective and one approach before you make each phone call.

Number your points for impact

Whether you're calling a newspaper editor to get a story or a venue owner to get a paying gig, consider using a number to indicate how many important points you plan to touch on.

Example: "Pat, I know you have a lot of bands that want press in your paper (or want to work at your club), but I'd like to mention three benefits you'd get from using us ..." People will listen more attentively when they know how many points they will hear – plus, it helps you organize your thoughts.

Give two positive choices when making your pitch

The worst thing you can do when marketing your music by phone is ask the other person to make a choice between "yes" and "no." In other words, if you were speaking with a radio station music director, it wouldn't be wise to say, "So, will you play my new single or not?" A question like that makes it too easy for the other person to say, "No."

Better: Instead, do a little research on the station's programs and show hosts. Then ask a question along the lines of, "Do you think this song would work better for you on Sarah's morning show or during Greg's new music show on Sunday night?" This way, you give the contact two choices – neither one of which is not playing your song. If you were speaking with a music business attorney seeking representation, you might ask, "Would you like me to overnight our CD and promo package to you today or email a link to our electronic press kit?"

Apply this method to conversations with venue owners, retailers, and other media people too.

Keep plugging away when you're on a roll

Let's be honest. There are times when we're "hot" and times we're "not." While we'd all like to be energetic and effective at all times (and there are ways to reach that productive state more often), sometimes it just doesn't happen. Therefore, take advantage of those times when you're on a roll by staying at it.

Example: Let's say you just got off the phone with a venue manager who finally booked your act into that long-awaited weekend headlining slot. You may be tempted to call your band mates and rejoice at the victory or sit for a while and dwell on your success.

Instead, pick up the phone and call another contact immediately. Strike while the music marketing iron is hot! Productivity has a funny way of multiplying when you're on a roll.

Use a music marketing log to stay on track

If you make even a minimal amount of phone calls to promote your music career, you know how easy it is to forget important details such as who you called, when you called them, what was discussed, and how you were supposed to follow up.

What you want to avoid is calling someone and saying, "Hello, Bill. Say, didn't I talk to you last month about doing a feature story on my band? Or was it for your review column? ... Oh, that's right. Anyway, did you ever get our new CD? I'm pretty sure I sent it out to you ..."

Solution: Use a music marketing log sheet for each contact you call. Print a fill-in-the-blank form that includes lines for name, company, email and street addresses, phone and fax numbers. Below that leave plenty of space for columns that list the date of contact, topics discussed, action you need to take next, and when you took that action.

Then print dozens of copies of the blank sheets and divide them in a three-ring binder into categories such as print media, radio, venues, record stores, distributors, etc. Start using these log sheets every time you communicate with someone about marketing your music, and jot down notes in the appropriate spaces. Of course, you can also come up with your own electronic version of these log sheets.

Bottom line: By using these marketing logs, everything you need to know about any contact is listed on only one page. And the next time you call someone you'll have the confidence to start the conversation by saying something like, "Hello, Bill. I'm following up on the conversation we had two weeks ago about my band's new release. You mentioned you might have room for a review in your December issue.

I mailed a CD to you on the 10th. Is there anything else I can do to help make that review happen?"

(You'll find a basic music marketing log sheet in the free worksheets that come with this book. Download a copy from worksheets.thebuzzfactor.com.)

Find out exactly what the person wants

Most people who market their music by phone like to pile on layer after layer of self-congratulatory nonsense. They beat their chests and tell some innocent victim how much they like themselves, using an endless stream of adjectives. Meanwhile, the contact waits on the other end of the phone for a chance to break in and tell the caller what he or she really needs to know.

Even though I've had to endure countless calls like this over the years, please spare the people you call from this torturous ritual. Instead, make it your goal to find out what your contact needs from you to make what you want materialize. While you should speak of your project in positive terms, don't jump headlong into a dissertation on your great qualities before first finding out what it is your contact is looking for.

Example: You might talk a music editor's ear off about your alternative band's new album. Little do you know, the editor just got out of a meeting in which the staff agreed they were covering too much local alternative music. What you also didn't know was that the editor was planning a story on band members with unique day jobs. Had you slowed down and asked a few questions, you might have discovered that. Then you could have let the editor know about your drummer, who is a parachute instructor.

It's always best to ask questions and find out what your contact's needs are. That way you'll open up a lot more opportunities for gigs, press and airplay – and get brushed off a lot less often.

Make sure you contact the right person

First, it should be a given that you uncover the names of the people who can help you (the proper editor, writer, music director, talent buyer, etc.) at the places you call. And if you get a name from a directory listing or through a suggestion from a friend, call the company and verify two things:

1) The person still works there and continues to hold the same title, and ...

2) You have the correct spelling and pronunciation of the person's name (recall the Bob Barker story I mentioned earlier)

In addition to that, it would help to investigate further and make sure the contact's duties truly relate to what you're going after. For instance, when I published my former music magazine, I carried the title of editor and publisher. And it's true that

I made the final decisions on what subjects were covered in the paper. Therefore, people seeking publicity naturally tended to ask for me when they called.

What they quickly discovered – that is, if they used the right approach – was that the magazine's production manager, not me, was the person responsible for handling callers who pitched story ideas.

Too many of these eager, exposure-seeking individuals made the mistake of asking for me instead of explaining who they were and why they were calling. Consequently, these generic PR calls rarely got returned. And the poor souls who placed them surely cursed the world and wondered why they were being cheated out of their share of publicity.

Lesson: Ask a couple of basic questions, explain your purpose for calling, and find out if the name you have is really the best person to contact. People will help you if you only let them.

Give honest compliments when appropriate

Use this one sparingly, because if it's not rendered with genuine appreciation, it could backfire. However, if you sincerely like the stand a writer took in a recent article, the new radio show a program director developed, or the remodeling that a venue owner just finished, tell them so.

Insight: This not only makes them feel good, but it shows them you're paying attention to what they're doing and are interested in more than just your own self-absorbed advancement.

Take the blame when the person doesn't understand

One thing you can count on is that there will be times when the contact on the other end of the line just doesn't comprehend your vision for a paid gig, a write-up, etc. Obviously, a bad move would be to condemn the person by barking, "Aren't you getting any of this?" or "Maybe if I speak slower you'll be able to keep up with me" (although you'll often be tempted to say just that).

At times like this, it's best to realize that the person might be distracted by something, is right in the middle of another project, or simply isn't up on the musical style or topic you're presenting. Remember, no one will be as interested in your music and career as much as you are.

Better approach: Be patient and offer positive remarks, such as:

- "Would there be a better time for me to call you back to talk about how my new single ended up in a movie soundtrack?" Or …

- "I'm sorry, I must not be clearly explaining how my band could bring an extra 100 people into your club next month."

Note that both of these statements include a benefit to the contact, as well as a polite way to clarify your pitch.

Grab their attention

Sometimes your contact's thoughts will wander. He or she simply won't be hanging on every word that comes out of your mouth during a phone conversation. One way to bring them back is to use an attention-getting statement. Here are a few good ones to try:

1) "Fran, if you don't remember anything else about this phone call, please remember this ..."

2) "Jim, if I had to give you the number one reason to give this band airplay, it would be this ..."

3) "Mary, I've never told anybody this before, but ..."

4) "Joe, in addition to everything we've talked about, there's one overriding reason we should be playing your nightclub on weekends ..."

5) "You know, the best thing I could do for you right now is this ..."

Warning: If you're going to set someone up for a convincing, eye-opening revelation, make sure what you reveal packs a mean punch.

The final point-blank approach

There comes a time when you've done seemingly everything in your power to book the gig, make the appointment, get the airplay ... and still your phone contact waffles around with vague reasons for not giving you what you want – without firmly saying he or she isn't interested.

At this point, the direct approach is the best. Here are four last-resort techniques:

1) "Nancy, I respect your time, so just be straight with me. What has to happen for you to move forward with the article?"

2) "John, we already have this much invested in making this club date a reality, why not get out your calendar right now and schedule it?"

3) "I've given you everything you need to add this song into rotation. Can we please take the next step and make it happen?"

4) "Fred, I need your help. What will it take to get this done?"

Important note: Use these final approaches only after you've:

- Supplied the contact with everything he or she has asked for

- Made at least a few initial contacts

- Been polite and professional throughout

- Pitched a number of specific ideas to help get what you want

- Kept the contact's interests foremost in mind

Yes, there is an important place for the telephone in your music promotion efforts. Use the ideas in this chapter to reach the right people, start meaningful relationships, and get more of what you want in the music business.

19 Things You Should Be Doing Right Now to Promote Your Music Better

There are literally thousands of strategies that successful songwriters, musicians and bands have used over the years to promote themselves more effectively. What follows are 19 techniques and ideas you can start using today to spread the word about your music. There are three key words in that last sentence. Two are *start using*; the third is *today*! Take those words to heart as you absorb these ideas and motivate yourself to put them into action.

At the very least, choose just one tactic from this chapter and get moving on it. Starting today!

1) Write a letter to the editor

Respond to a music-related topic in your local newspaper or a national magazine. Work in a mention of your band and website. As long as you have an insightful comment and are subtle about plugging yourself, chances are good it will end up in print or online.

2) Use strong headlines to promote yourself

Album cover graphics and other artwork are great, but research shows that bold, attention-getting headlines (with more details following in the smaller-size body copy) pull the most response from ads, fliers, posters, and web pages.

3) Include complete contact info on everything

Bios and press releases get separated from CDs and photos. Don't leave anything to chance. Include your name, address, phone, email, and website address on every piece of marketing communication you send out or give away.

4) Commit to connecting with one fan at a time

Unlike the major labels, you don't have to market to millions of people and sell 250,000 copies of your album to be successful. Commit to working at the grassroots level, connecting with one new fan at a time. At first, you'll have 10 followers. Then 100, then 500, and eventually 1,000 and more. Take the personal approach of slowly but surely building up your community of supportive fans.

5) Use testimonials and positive review quotes

Don't just use your press clippings and fan mail to impress mom and dad. Positive quotes from third-party sources add lots of clout toward your efforts to get media exposure, airplay, gigs, and more. And don't just wait for them to come to you. Ask radio, newspaper, venue, and other industry people you know for a line you can use in your press kit. Make this an ongoing activity.

6) Ask politely but firmly for action

Whether your goal is to get an album review, radio airplay or a paid gig, always make sure to *ask* for what you want. Don't apologize. Don't beat around the bush. Don't wimp out. Just ask! And do it pleasantly and confidently.

7) Create and distribute take-one boxes

Keep an eye out for small cardboard boxes you can recycle into "take one" containers. Print small handout fliers that promote the availability of your new release or dates of your upcoming shows. Place these in the boxes, which should be covered with artwork and text that says: "Hey You! Take one of these" (or something more clever). Then ask local record store, coffee shop or retail store managers if you can place these unique boxes in their establishments. Chances are, you'll be the only artist in town doing this.

8) Offer a tongue-in-cheek report or survey

Take a poll of your fans, interview people on the streets, or just act as if you have ... it doesn't matter. This isn't scientific research, but it can be a fun way to hook the media into covering you.

Example: Let's say you came up with the results of a survey titled "The Top 10 Reasons Local Music Fans Watch the Jerry Springer Show" or "What Toledo Nightclub-Goers Think of Madonna as a Mother – Startling Survey Results!" If it's funny and timely enough, a lot of the newspapers, magazines and Internet sources you contact will mention your survey. Some may even run all of your survey results – while plugging the source: *you*. Also include this survey in a newsletter to your fans.

9) Present a music-related contest

In the same way that surveys and tongue-in-cheek reports (listed in the previous tip) can lead to public awareness, so can contests bring you valuable exposure. They can either be serious (a Guitar Player Challenge, your basic Battle of the Bands) or more light-hearted (Stupid Musician Tricks, the World's Largest Twister Game).

One guy in my hometown presents an annual Night of a Thousand Spoons, during which hordes of musicians play ... you guessed it, spoons. And it gets press every year. The best contests, though, will tie in nicely with your band name, album title, or overall musical identity. Find one that works for you.

10) Have an attitude/take a stand

Musicians who try to be all things to all people usually come up short when promoting themselves. The most successful artists know who they are, know what they stand for, and aren't afraid of alienating segments of the population when expressing themselves. Sure, you may rub some music fans the wrong way. But the fans who do identify with you will back you all the way.

Warning: Think twice before you decide to express something that will shock people. Make sure you are doing it because you truly feel that way and the thing you say or do really represents who you are. Don't do it merely for the sake of being controversial. It could backfire on you if it's not authentic.

11) Get on other artists' mailing lists

Countless songwriters and bands are doing all kinds of things to promote themselves. Most of them use ho-hum methods. But every now and then you run across a real promotional gem. Wouldn't you like to be aware of those gems more often? Get on the mailing lists of other artists you admire. Start observing how successful groups and record labels promote themselves. "Borrow" some of the better ideas and discard the rest.

12) Build a powerful reference library

I've become quite leery of the phrase "Knowledge is power." Not only is it overused, but the truth is, knowledge without taking the steps to use it creatively and effectively is useless. That said, I still encourage you to absorb as much info as you can on the music business and other topics that are important to you. The best way to do that is to build a personal empowerment reference library.

The bookcases in my home resemble the how-to and self-help sections of a major bookstore. My shelves are stocked not only with music industry-related titles, they're also filled with volumes on publicity, small business marketing, time management, sales techniques, positive thinking, nutrition, spirituality, and much more.

My personal library serves as a constant reminder of the areas I need to stay sharp on, and I quite frequently pull out a book for a quick refresher course on whatever topic I need help with. You'd be wise to do the same thing.

13) Follow up on everything

This should be a no-brainer, but you'd be surprised by the number of people who pay lip service to the concept of follow-through and still end up overlooking it. The idea here is simple: If you tell someone you're going to send a package, for example ... make sure you do it! Once the package is sent, follow up with a phone call or email to make sure the person received it. Wait a couple of weeks (or however long is appropriate for the situation) and contact the person again to get the status of the review, feature story, gig, or whatever it is you're after.

Insight: Don't expect other people or the whims of fate to take care of your career. Grab the reins and stay on top of your promotional activities. Doing so will virtually guarantee that good things will come your way.

14) Get the correct spelling of people's names

If you've heard me share this story before, here it is again: I've grown tired of getting mail and phone calls directed to Bob Barker. My last name is Baker. It always has been and always will be. I am not a game show host. And if I were, I'd much prefer *Wheel of Fortune* over *The Price Is Right*.

The point: Anyone who refers to me as Bob Barker starts off with a serious mark against them. It tells me they haven't done their homework and are probably rushing through the motions of promoting themselves. So my advice to you is slow down and make sure you:

- Have the name of a specific person to contact

- Are certain he or she is the proper person you need to be contacting

- Get the exact spelling (and pronunciation) of the person's name

15) Send thank-you notes

This is a simple act, but it really does make a difference. When a writer does a story on your band or when a disc jockey plays one of your songs during her show, send a quick note of thanks. These small acts of random kindness do make an impression on the people receiving them. And it just may cause your music connections to have a cozier attitude toward you the next time you approach them for a favor.

Example: When the Borders bookstores went out of business, I sent a thank-you email to a manager who had done a lot for me and many other local authors. She had worked at Borders for more than 12 years. She responded and said I was one of only two authors who took the time to thank her for her years of service. See how easy it is to express your appreciation and stand out from the crowd at the same time?

Another thing you can do to stand out is send a real card. Buy a box of inexpensive thank-you cards and have them handy whenever someone does something to help you. Or have a template set up on your computer and personalize each card as you print it.

16) Practice unselfish communication

Success in the music business has as much to do with the quality of your relationships as it does the quality of your music. One of your goals should be to make friends and fans of people who are in a real position to help further your career.

But a friendship is a two-way transaction. If you only communicate with someone when you need something from him or her, the relationship is not on a balanced, solid ground. That's why you should get in the habit of calling, mailing, and emailing your music contacts occasionally when you want nothing from them at all. Call to ask how a recent holiday went, to wish them a happy birthday, to pass along helpful information you came across that might interest them, etc.

Key: You should always have a specific objective in mind any time you communicate with someone, but your objective doesn't always have to be self-serving.

17) Describe your identity in 15 words or less

When you finally get a music editor or program director on the phone, he may very well ask, "So what kind of music do you play?" How will you respond? By hem-hawing around about how unique your sound is and how you "hate labels"? Don't get caught in this trap.

You should be able to define your music and identity in 15 words or less. There are two primary reasons to do this:

1) So you can quickly communicate your sound and identity to media sources, industry people, and potential fans alike

2) So you can use it as a gauge by which to focus all of your songs, titles, artwork, photos, ads, and more around a consistent theme

People (including you) shouldn't be confused about what they get from you and your music.

For more details on this topic, read about Brand Identity Statements in Chapter 3.

18) Supply questions to radio and TV interviewers

When you get invited to do a radio or TV interview – whether it's for the local college radio station, public access TV, or VH1 – you're being handed a great chance to get your message out to the public and connect with thousands of new fans. Don't blow the opportunity by sending a watered-down, ambiguous message.

Interviewers might have good intentions, but if they're not given a road map, there's no telling what tangent they might veer off on while speaking to you on the air. That's why supplying them with a list of questions and topics can help keep your message on track.

Of course, even when you do offer suggested questions, the interviewer may ignore them. When this happens, find a sensible, non-threatening way to steer the conversation back to the specific ideas you want to get across regarding who you are and what you play. Publicists often call these primary ideas you want to communicate via the media "talking points." Whatever you call them, it's important to know what you want to talk about long before you show up for an interview.

19) Write down a plan of action

While you want to be flexible enough to take advantage of promotional opportunities that spring up unexpectedly, nothing beats having a solid plan of action. And writing down your plan gives it substance. To help craft the best plan, ask yourself the following questions:

- What specific message do I want to get across to music fans and industry people?

- What are the best ways to get that idea across?

- What creative tactics should I pursue first in my effort to promote my music using this idea?

- What should I do next?

Write down your answers to these questions and develop a more refined plan. Then get busy and take the first step. The plan is always subject to change, but simply having one in the first place gets you moving toward your goals. Action, energy and movement lead to new opportunities, open doors, and unexpected good fortune.

For more on effective planning and goal setting, turn back to Chapter 2.

Action step: As I encouraged you to do at the beginning of this chapter, pick at least one of these 19 promotional ideas and start working on it today!

Chapter 20

Often-Overlooked Promotion Strategies You Should Be Using to Market Your Music

Have you been in a marketing rut lately? Are you having a tough time coming up with new and innovative promotion ideas? You won't be for long. Soak up the ideas in this chapter and get moving. Every day that passes without you actively promoting your music is lost time. So read on … then get busy!

Music marketing and the state of your fans

In this first section, let's talk about sizzle and steak. You've most likely heard the old advertising credo "Sell the sizzle, not the steak." It's another way of saying "Push customer benefits, not product features." This mantra has been repeated time and time again in marketing circles for decades. Unfortunately, most people continue to ignore the wisdom.

To see how you stack up in this area, I'll give you a quick test. Answer these two questions:

- What business are you in?

- What do you really offer your fans?

If you answered, "I'm in the music business, and I offer them my CDs, merchandise and live concerts," you're dead wrong. Items such as T-shirts, CDs and concerts are pure features. And features are simply things you technically do or produce in the course of creating your music. Sure, you must focus on these things when you create them. But they're not what your fans focus on when they spend money on your recordings and live shows.

Question: So … what *do* fans buy? Here's the answer (and write this down in a visible place and remind yourself of it often): The real reason consumers buy music is to experience the emotional and physical "state change" that occurs within them – because of the music you create. For instance …

- High-energy music pumps up its followers and gets their adrenaline flowing.

- New Age and acoustic music soothes the minds and bodies of listeners.

- Sad love songs remind romantic folks of a similar event in their lives.

- Ethnic music helps people connect with their roots.

- Oldies bring back memories and feelings of the good old days.

- Classical music awes and inspires.

Regardless of the style or genre, music touches people on both an emotional and physical level. The state of the listener before hearing your music is decidedly different from what it is during the hearing (or watching) of it. State changes add adventure and excitement to our lives – which is exactly why so many people turn to sex, drugs, alcohol, and extreme sports to do the same thing for them.

Never forget this. And start asking yourself, "What kind of state change does my music inspire in my fans?" When you're creating, by all means focus on the music, the albums, and the concerts. But forget all that when it comes to communicating with your fans – and start concentrating on how your music affects people on a deeper level.

Key questions: When it comes to sending out marketing messages about your music, what's going to get the best response? Talking about your "new album, now available on iTunes"? Or reminding people of the real reason they're going to buy it? Meaning the emotional and physical payoff they get when they spend a few dollars or more on your music.

In case you didn't know it, you're no longer in the music business. You're now in the "state change" business – especially when it comes to marketing your music.

How to use pain and pleasure to promote yourself

Let me ask you another question: What are the two major forces that motivate human beings to act? You might be tempted to say things like "money and sex" or "security and respect."

Yes, those are motivating factors, but let's break them down into the two most basic components. Here they are: Human beings either want to move closer to pleasure or away from pain. That's it. The motivation behind everything you or any other person does can be broken down into one or both of these categories: getting pleasure or avoiding pain.

Examples: Eating helps you avoid hunger pains and at times enjoy a fine meal (sorry, a Big Mac doesn't count). You're inspired to make money to avoid the pain of not paying your bills and get the pleasure of treating yourself to the things you want.

Perhaps you play music to get the pleasure of creating and the recognition that comes when you share it with others. Or maybe you play music to avoid the pain of not having an outlet for your creative urges.

Pleasure motivations occur when people aspire to a higher level or to experience one of those feel-good "state changes." Pain motivations occur when we want to eliminate a current physical or emotional nuisance, or when we want to avoid a potential loss we believe may happen in the near future.

The truth: Of these two motivators, pain is the strongest. People tend to grieve over a perceived loss more than a gain. For instance, which would be more intense: Your level of happiness at finding $100, or your level of frustration at losing $100? Most people would feel the loss more intensely.

Marketers use both of these factors all the time. For example, weight loss clinics and diet book publishers have two marketing options. One, they can concentrate on the pleasure people will get once they reach a desired lower weight. Or two, they can remind people how unhappy they are now and how that pain can be removed if they only sign up or buy the book. Of the two approaches, the second is the strongest motivator.

So how does this apply to marketing your music? Take a look at the emotional, physical and spiritual impact your music has on fans. Does it pump them up? Calm them down? Make them feel connected? Nostalgic? Romantic? Inspired? What's the real payoff your fans get from your music? By now you should know what that payoff is.

Now take those qualities and express them in both pleasure-gaining and pain-avoiding terms. Here are some examples:

A high-energy rock band

Pleasure: We'll get you pumped up and feeling alive and energetic.

Pain: Tired of your mundane nine-to-five work routine? Sick of sissy pop rock when you turn on the radio? We have the antidote for your blahs right here.

An acoustic folk act

Pleasure: Our songs will soothe your mind with catchy, mellow guitar melodies and make you smile.

Pain: With your fast-paced schedule, the last thing you need is more of that angst-ridden junk you always hear on the radio. Our music is your solution.

An avant-garde jazz trio

Pleasure: Exciting rhythms and invigorating instrumentation await you on our new album. Give your ears the musical spice they hunger for.

Pain: Sure, you could continue to be lulled to sleep by the dull, predictable sounds of most new jazz acts. Or you could give yourself some much-deserved relief and treat yourself to real music from seasoned jazz pros.

A romantic balladeer

Pleasure: Snuggle up with your honey and sway to these timeless songs – guaranteed to supercharge your love life.

Pain: Has your love life been in a rut? Do you have trouble getting in the mood? The romantic relief you need awaits you on my new album of soothing love songs.

Get the idea? Your best bet is to use both pain and pleasure tactics when writing your music marketing materials. Hit people from both angles. It will help drive home the benefits of your music and give your fans (and potential fans) one good reason after another to give your music a try. And, it will keep them coming back for more of the pleasure-gaining and pain-avoiding goodies you have waiting for them.

Identify your image

Musicians who choose to portray a certain image often attempt to mislead the music-buying public. And music consumers show their displeasure by staying away from your shows and new album in droves. Having an "image" implies something phony – a facade that tries to manipulate the people exposed to it.

Instead of trying to communicate your image, start marketing your "identity." An identity is an honest expression of what your music and personality are all about. I know this may seem like a nit-picking argument over semantics, since many people use these terms interchangeably. But if you focus on clarifying your "identity," it forces you to send a more honest message regarding your music.

And that kind of honesty breeds confidence and attracts fans like magnets.

Grab attention – with a purpose

Before you fall in love with a crazy new promotion scheme, consider this: People will remember the most fascinating part of your marketing but not necessarily your band or new release. Of course, this all depends on what the most fascinating aspect is. If you display an eye-catching photo or piece of artwork on your website or fliers, people may remember the visual image but not your band name. If you use a witty headline, they may remember the humor but not your musical identity.

Reality: Music consumers are first and foremost interested in the benefit they get from the artists they support. So if you want to interest them, relate your marketing pitch directly to their needs. And do it in a way that makes your band or new release the most fascinating part of the message.

For instance, one record label ran a print ad that still has me scratching my head. A collage of bizarre artwork took up half of the ad; the other half was filled with small, hard-to-read text. I think this ad was promoting several of the label's releases, but I'm not sure. I know that this company specializes in unconventional, experimental sounds, but this experimental marketing ploy didn't help get the message across.

A half-page ad from Hannibal Records, on the other hand, does a nice job of using humor to get its point made. The headline reads, "Did you hear the one about the Cuban piano player, the Tibetan nun, and the Finnish accordionist?" The smaller subhead underneath explains, "It's no joke: They've made three must-have new world music albums for Hannibal."

Each album then has a one-sentence description and that's it – short, sweet, interesting, and effective. Just like all good music marketing efforts should be!

Demo strategies that set your music apart

Whether you want to attract the attention of a publisher, record label, music magazine or radio station, you need to find ways to make your music submissions stand out. Here are two ideas few others are using:

1) Several years ago, as I was going through submissions to an annual music conference, I came across a CD that featured snippets of about eight songs from one band. Each song faded out after about 30 seconds and the next song began. I got a quick earful of this group's music without getting bored or having to fast-forward through the disc.

I believe that, in the right situations, this sampling presentation can be an effective one. It gives you more bang for your buck, especially if you make the recipient aware of the time-saving benefits of this format.

Strategy: Include a short letter that states something like: "You're busy. You haven't got time to listen to every note of every song that comes across your desk. That's why we've made it easy for you to enjoy a three-minute sampling of our six best songs. That's all it takes. Three minutes. And you're done. If you like what you hear, contact us for our full-length album ..."

If more artists used this approach, they'd probably see a better response to their promotional efforts.

2) This second demo submission technique could work well along with the first one or by itself. It involves recording a personalized voice message at the beginning of each CD or MP3 file you send. Let's say you plan to send the six-song sampler mentioned above. Make the first 30 seconds a recording of your voice greeting the specific person it is meant for. Yes, this tactic will take a little extra time for you to record individual messages for each contact.

The CD or MP3 file should be delivered with a note saying: "I recorded a personal message just for you on the first 30 seconds of this recording. I think this is something you'll want to hear."

How it works: Once the person's curiosity is teased and he or she hits the play button, your recorded message might say: "Hi, Pat. This is Fred from the band Green Slime. I really enjoy your columns in *The Weekly Music Rag*, especially the piece you did on (insert any detailed reference, as long as it's genuine). I know you're busy and are probably sick of opening mail, so I thought I'd give you a change of pace with this voice cover letter. The rest of this disc contains... (here you can borrow wording used in the music sampler example above)."

The reason these two tactics work is because they meet the two most important criteria for marketing music:

- They keep the recipient's limited time foremost in mind.

- They are truly different from the norm.

Street smarts

Here's a good example of a fresh angle for a compilation CD. Clay Dog Records put out *Street Dreams*, a collection of music from some of Chicago's more visible street musicians – recorded live at the corners and subway stops they frequent.

Lesson: If you put together a compilation, make sure there's a logical and appealing thread that holds it all together. Saying "Here's a bunch of cool bands" won't be the strongest idea. But a lot of cool music centered around a common theme might get more attention.

The same thing goes for promoting a single artist. Always keep your identity consistent. When people see your fliers, post cards, album artwork or website, they should know without a doubt that it's all coming from the same artist. You can do this by keeping your logo, typefaces, and the tone of your wording consistent. This might seem bland and repetitious to the person designing the material, but if you always change the look and feel of your marketing, you will confuse your fans.

What would you rather have: a lot of people who know exactly what your music is about, or a lonely portfolio of disjointed press kits, photos and artwork?

College fan payoff

The Dirges is a band made up of students who attended Pennsylvania State University. The band's three independently released albums sold a total of 10,000 copies in three years.

"Think about it," says guitarist/keyboardist Steve Bodner, "ten thousand people graduate from this college each year and move to places all across the country. We go right along with them."

Are you taking advantage of the college market?

Music promotion on wheels

Organic Records has a specially designed flatbed truck that travels city to city to gain exposure for its artists. The acts can perform live right on the truck or simply give away samplers and promotional items from it at special events.

Can you develop a fresh method of exposing your music to new groups of people?

Sunny skies in the forecast

Artist Bryan Duncan released an album called *Blue Skies*. To make the most of the album title, his record label ran radio ads sponsoring weather reports in key regions of the country. Duncan also did radio interviews during which he read the local weather forecast on the air. You can bet there weren't many other artists taking this approach.

Is there anything about your album title or band name that can be transformed into a creative marketing strategy?

Cover up

Tired of being denied radio airplay because stations prefer to pump out familiar music to the masses? One solution: Stop fighting and go with the status quo. Australian band the Clouds received some attention when it recorded a cover of Glen Campbell's "Wichita Lineman."

"It's a beautiful song," says bassist Patricia Young. "Not only that, it's a lot easier to pick up airplay with familiar material."

Might there be a cover song that you can put your own fresh spin on? (See Chapter 8 for details on how Pomplamoose and Karmin used cover songs successfully.)

More expansive ideas: On a recent trip to the library, I checked out Jay Conrad Levinson's book *Guerrilla Marketing Attack*. Like the other books in Levinson's "Guerrilla" series, this volume is packed with dozens of usable business-building tactics.

I've taken the liberty of giving some of the concepts from the book a musical slant with the following three tips:

Use eight stamps instead of one

As you know, people are bombarded with mail (both electronic and physical). Music editors, program directors, managers, talent bookers – they all receive an avalanche of unsolicited mail. One creative, low-cost way to make your physical package stand out is to use more stamps than anyone else is using.

Instead of sending your letter with a single first-class stamp, why not stick on several stamps that all add up to 45 cents (or whatever the current postage rate is)? Who would fail to open a letter with eight stamps on it? You might even write a funny phrase like "We're hoping for your stamp of approval" on the outside of the envelope.

Arrange for positive picketers to demonstrate

The idea here is to gather a group of your supporters to demonstrate outside of an establishment. But instead of protesting, these people would carry signs that praise your music or new release. Each sign would have a different review quote, ringing endorsement, or photo.

Key: This marketing tactic is so fresh and unexpected, it just might generate a lot of favorable publicity in the area. You'd be wise to get the blessings of the venue manager or storeowner before proceeding with this one. But with the potential exposure it could generate, you should have no problem finding at least one establishment to actively participate in the mock picket.

Embrace your customers for a lifelong relationship

Most music marketers don't see the ongoing value of a single customer. They sell a new fan a $12 CD and take pride in making a $9 or $10 profit. But the guerrilla music marketer sees it differently.

He or she knows that with proper care and attention, a single new fan can be worth far more over the course of many years. Not only will that fan buy future releases and attend numerous shows, but this person will also tell others about this great artist that treats him or her so well.

These new, referred fans will also buy a lot of albums and pay the cover at many live concerts. A single album sale (with a $10 profit) has the potential to be worth 10 to 20 times that over several years. That is, if you caress and pamper your fans (figuratively, of course) and show them you really care.

Do this: Use the often-overlooked ideas in this chapter to promote and sell your music more effectively.

Final Guerrilla Music Marketing Thoughts

Congratulations!

You've just accomplished what the majority of musicians never get around to. You made a decision to feed your mind with potent ideas that will, when acted upon, lead to greater notoriety and higher levels of success.

Most musicians wallow in obscurity and complain about the sad state of their local music scene or the industry at large. But guess what? You won't do that.

Why? Because you now know that attitude is everything, that what you think about expands, and that you have a lot more control over your destiny than most people give themselves credit for.

We live in an incredible era of self-empowerment and opportunity. I hope, after reading this book, you now realize that and will use this knowledge to share your music more fully with the world.

If you haven't been there lately, I encourage you to visit my website at **www.TheBuzzFactor.com**. There you'll find dozens of resources to help you get exposure, book more gigs, attract fans, and sell more music.

While you're on the site, be sure to subscribe to my free *Buzz Factor* ezine, read my music promotion blog, listen to my Artist Empowerment Radio podcast, and watch my free marketing video clips. All of these resources deliver a regular dose of music marketing tips and inspiring ideas that reinforce what you've learned in this book.

Of course, you should also download the free worksheets that come with this book. For that just visit **worksheets.thebuzzfactor.com**.

I wish you success in all that you do. May all of your dreams come true, both on and off the stage!

–Bob

Special Recognition Section

When I launched this updated edition of the book, I used my own version of the "fan funding" method. I gave people access to the book's content before it was completely written, designed and printed. And I gave special perks to those who ordered it in advance.

(I encourage you to expand your thinking in the same way and consider new ways you can write, record, produce, promote, and share your music with your fans.)

I want to thank the following people who took me up on my pre-publication offer. I applaud and recognize them for playing an important role in the success of this book!

Don Campbell, Don Campbell Music, www.doncampbellmusic.com

Waverider Mobile, www.waveridermobile.com

Marius Noss Gundersen, Classical Guitarist, www.marius-gundersen.no

Gracie Vandiver, Mother Knows Best Media, www.MKBmedia.com

Demian E Yumei, DreamSinger, www.keepingthedream.com

JT, www.musichitsface.com

Jason Ayres, www.jasonayres.com

Matt J. Miller, Anton Music Productions, www.ampmilwaukee.com

Walt Pitts, Versatile Professional Mobile Music, LLC, www.WaltPitts.com

Massimo de Majo, www.massimodemajo.com

Kevin Downing, Kevin Downing's Guitar School, www.guitar.co.nz

Roland Battistini, Composer, www.rolandbattistini.tv

Vulcano Records

Alain Galarneau, www.alaingalarneau.com

Fern Michonski, Fern's Music / Fern Forest Enterprises, www.FernsMusicForKids.com

Junshuo Hou, Liquid Tension Music, www.liquidtensionmusic.com

Descried, www.descried.com

Sylvia Bennett, Out of Sight Music, www.SylviaBennett.com

Peter Woolston, Music With a Mission to Rock Your World,
www.peterwoolston.com

Megrov, www.megrov.com

Sunny Williams, www.sunny-williams.com

Mark! Andrew, Mark! Andrew Galaxy, www.markandrewgalaxy.com

Kita-Simone, www.kitasimone.com

Katherine Moller, www.katherinemoller.ca

Bryan Dean, Bryan Dean Trio, www.BryanDeanTrio.com

David Boswell, www.davidboswell.com

Ahveekhy Ben BinahYah, Sound of Paradise, www.deliverance-music.org

Wendy Waller, www.wendywaller.com

Mary McKay, Soul Music Revival, www.marymckay.ca

T Dawn, Beyond the Dawn Radio, www.tdawn.com

Alexy Guerer, Alexy & The Other Side, www.alexymusic.com

† The Deacon †, Mama's Dirty Li'l Secret, www.RockHardRockSexy.com

Christine A Rose, www.frissonentertainment.com

Allan Rufus, Personal Development through Self Discovery, www.allanrufus.org

Mark de Smit, Mark on Sound, www.markonsound.com

Steve Lentz, Driven/F.O.G., www.drivenrocks.com

Sue Straw, Sue Straw Music, www.SueStrawMusic.com

Diamondisc Audio, Doug Diamond, www.diamondiscaudio.com

Pete Cohan, www.TheBlazers.net

www.Magna.fm

Tristan Pearson, Clockwork Records, www.clockworkrecords.com

Kristian Jackson, www.kristianjackson.com

Chris Rollason, The Hair Thieves, www.hairthieves.com

Phil Hooton, Zeffa, www.ZeffaMusic.com

Karyn Ellis, Mathilde's Home Production, www.karynellis.com

Steve Mulry, Black Label Australia, www.blacklabelaustralia.com.au

Oxaï Roura, www.oxairoura.com

Chris Wesley, www.chriswesley.com

Kate McLennan and Noel Tardy, www.spiritrunnersmusic.com

Kaleo Wheeler, Musical Storyteller, www.kaleowheeler.com

Jason Hayward, Spinoza Gambit, www.spinozagambit.com

Lou Volpe, Lou Volpe Jazz Guitar, www.louvolpejazz.com

Igor Markitantov, Music Promo Projects, www.muspp.com

Richard Dole, www.richarddole.com

Gloryan, www.gloryan-music.com

Zubi d'Nova, www.zubionline.com

Derrek Michael, Elm & Olympia, www.elmandolympia.com

Marcus Macadi, www.marcusmacadi.com

Mark Gosney, Media Composing Unlimited, www.media-composing-unlimited.com

Duane "DCT" Thorpe, Urbanizm Music, www.sonicskillz.com

Denise Ford, Denise Ford Music & Promotion, www.denisefordmusic.ca

Tammy Griffith, Vocal Strategies LLC, www.vocalstrategies.com

Laurena Marrone, Grit PR & Promotion, LLC, www.gritpr.com

Jonathan Ramsey, www.jonathanramsey.com

Yvonne Smith, Crater Rock Music, LLC, www.craterrockmusic.com

Jim Crozier, JacrozierMusic, www.jimcrozier.com

Paul Taneja, Pinto and the Bean, www.pintoandthebean.com

Deanne Matley, www.deannematley.com

Parkway Sound Records, www.parkwaysoundrecords.com

Rick Honeyboy Hart, Honeyboy, www.RickHoneyboyHart.com

Nick Bukuvalas, www.NickRocks.com

Rosenthol Curtis, Tha Yo, www.thayo.co

Mijail Kabadjov, Milo Kaih and The Grantholders, www.thegrantholders.com

Hans Timmermans, Budha Building, www.budhabuilding.com

Dave Halls, www.davehalls.com

Jawanza Kobie, www.JawanzaKobie.com

For more of Bob Baker's music marketing tips and tools, visit

www.TheBuzzFactor.com

www.MusicPromotionBlog.com

www.Bob-Baker.com/podcast

www.MusicMarketingBooks.com

You'll also find Bob on ...

www.Twitter.com/MrBuzzFactor

www.Facebook.com/BobBakerFanPage

www.YouTube.com/MrBuzzFactor

www.Linkedin.com/in/buzzfactor

www.Google.com/profiles/MrBuzzFactor

Want to publish (or promote) your own book?

www.FullTimeAuthor.com

www.IndieBookPromotion.com

Finally, to see some of Bob's artwork (yes, he's a visual artist too)

www.PopRockArtStudio.com

Lightning Source UK Ltd.
Milton Keynes UK
UKOW07f2258100916

282680UK00015B/261/P